The Logic of Mergers

*The competitive market in corporate control
in theory and practice*

BRIAN CHIPLIN

*Professor of Industrial Economics and
Director of the Nottingham Institute of Financial Studies,
University of Nottingham*

and

MIKE WRIGHT

*Lecturer in Industrial Economics and
Director of the Centre for Management Buy-out Research,
University of Nottingham*

Published by
THE INSTITUTE OF ECONOMIC AFFAIRS

First published in April 1987

by

THE INSTITUTE OF ECONOMIC AFFAIRS
2 Lord North Street, Westminster,
London SW1P 3LB

© THE INSTITUTE OF ECONOMIC AFFAIRS 1987

ISSN 0073-2818

ISBN 0-255 36199-8

Printed in Great Britain by
GORON PRO-PRINT CO LTD
6 Marlborough Road, Churchill Industrial Estate, Lancing, W. Sussex
Text set in 'Monotype' Baskerville

CONTENTS

[3]

FIGURES

PREFACE

The *Hobart Papers* are intended to contribute a stream of authoritative, independent and lucid analyses to the understanding and application of economics to private and to government activity. The characteristic theme has been the best use of scarce resources and how it can be achieved in markets within an appropriate framework of laws and institutions or, where markets cannot work, in other ways. Since the alternative to the market in the real world is the state, and both are imperfect, the choice between them effectively turns on a judgement of the comparative consequences of 'market failure' and 'government failure'.

Mergers, or takeovers, are—and, as *Hobart Paper 107* makes clear, have always been—an essential part of the process of growth in any economy that attempts to satisfy consumer choice through making the best allocation of economic resources. Equally, however, there has always been unease and criticism of many aspects of the merger movement, in particular a fear that it may bring about too great a degree of concentration and may also force companies to sacrifice long-term development plans in order to pay out higher dividends as a short-term protection against take-over.

In 1986-87 a number of large and contested bids involving prominent companies led to these and other criticisms being more widely and forcefully put forward. Competition policy, it was said, should be less indulgent and City investing institutions should be persuaded to use their influence positively to strengthen existing managements rather than passively to accept takeover offers from acquisitive companies, which in a few cases resorted to doubtful practices in trying to make their bid successful.

This objection was anticipated 27 years ago in an early *Hobart Paper* by Mr Anthony Vice:

'The balance sheet for take-overs . . . shows that general advantages may be marred by specific abuses'.[1]

[1] Anthony Vice, *Balance Sheet for Take-overs*, Hobart Paper 3, IEA, 1960.

The *techniques* used in some takeover battles, notably Guinness/ Distillers, may have left much to be desired, but the case for takeovers remains a strong one.

Too much should not be expected of an ideally-designed legal framework to smooth away all these difficulties unless legislators can resolve a central dilemma, namely, that if particular mergers are to be judged by general laws there can be no allowance for individual circumstances where cases differ—a problem discussed by several speakers at an IEA seminar in November 1972.[2] The preference of that meeting and of this *Hobart Paper* is that we should broadly keep to our 'case by case' approach in competition policy.

It was to assess these problems and indicate the way forward in such a complex field, that the IEA commissioned a study from Professor Brian Chiplin and Dr Mike Wright, drawing on their extensive research at the Institute of Financial Studies in the University of Nottingham. They were invited to stand back from immediate events and to put into perspective the role and consequences of what they call the market for corporate control between competing management teams. One conclusion that emerges is that it is the *threat* of a takeover that provides the most effective spur to efficiency. The danger therefore is that this discipline could only be weakened by excessive legislation or regulation.

Of particular interest is the authors' study of management buy-outs and divestment as ways in which companies can bring together the best configuration of assets to implement their corporate strategy.

The debate about takeovers will continue for many years yet. The Institute is pleased to present this *Hobart Paper* as a valuable contribution to that debate whilst, as is customary, dissociating its Trustees, Directors and Advisers from the authors' conclusions.

March 1987   JOHN B. WOOD

---

[1] Published as *Mergers, Take-overs and the Structure of Industry*, IEA Readings No. 10, 1973.

THE AUTHORS

BRIAN CHIPLIN is Professor of Industrial Economics and Head of the Department of Industrial Economics, Accountancy and Insurance at the University of Nottingham. He is also Director of the Nottingham Institute of Financial Studies and Co-Director of the University of Nottingham Institute of Management Studies. He has been visiting Professor at the State University of New York at Buffalo and the University of California, Irvine. He has written on financial markets, sex discrimination, labour market policies, merger policy, the economics of crime, and various aspects of industrial organisation. He is co-author of *Can Workers Manage?* (IEA Hobart Paper No. 77, 1977). His books include: *Personal Financial Markets* (Philip Allan, 1987); *Discrimination at the Workplace* (Cambridge University Press, 1982); *The Economics of Advertising* (Holt Reinhart and Winston, 1981); and *Acquisitions and Mergers: Government Policy in Europe* (Wilton House/Financial Times, 1975).

DR MIKE WRIGHT is Lecturer in Industrial Economics and Director of the Centre for Management Buy-out Research at the University of Nottingham. He was educated at New Mills Grammar School, Derbyshire, the University of Durham, and the University of Nottingham. He has published numerous articles in professional and academic journals on management buy-outs, divestment, competition policy, nationalised industries, information systems, building societies and financial services. He is the author of several books, most notably *Competition Policy, Profitability and Growth* (with D. P. O'Brien, W. S. Howe and R. J. O'Brien) (1979); *Management Buy-outs* (with J. Coyne) (1986); *Divestment and Strategic Change* (with J. Coyne) (1986); *Spicer and Pegler's Management Buy-outs* (with A. Mills and J. Coyne) (1987); *The Future of the Building Societies* (with T. Watkins) (1986); and *Marketing Financial Services* (with T. Watkins) (1986).

[9]

ACKNOWLEDGEMENTS

The authors would like to thank Professor Dennis O'Brien, Professor John Pickering, David Thompson and Professor Basil Yamey for their helpful comments and advice.

B.C.
M.W.

I. INTRODUCTION

'Merger Mania', 'Merger Mayhem', 'Bid Fever': these are just some examples of headlines in the British press in 1986 as a number of large British companies became the subject of takeover bids.[1] Concern over the implications of such mergers led the Secretary of State for Trade and Industry to announce in June 1986 a review of the law and policy on mergers. He stated that although existing competition laws had operated well, merger policy had attracted attention in recent months and the review would investigate both the scope for changes in policy under existing legislation, and the desirability of changes in the law.[2] Mergers and merger policy are thus an issue of considerable topical interest; the aim of this *Hobart Paper* is to place the current merger wave in context; to review the issues involved; and to suggest implications for policy.

The following questions will be examined:

1. What is the nature of current merger activity?
2. What part do mergers play in the restructuring of firms and industries?
3. Are mergers an efficient way to ensure that assets are employed in their best uses and operated to their best advantage?
4. What is the role of institutional investors and do pressures for short-term performance operate at the expense of the long-term interests of firms and the economy?
5. How have financial and legal innovations affected the merger process and what consequences do they have for the interested parties and the economy in general?
6. What is the appropriate role for merger policy?

---

[1] Strictly speaking, a takeover occurs when one company acquires control (usually 50 per cent or more of the equity shares) of another; a merger is where two companies (say, A and B) amalgamate to form a new legal entity (C). In this *Hobart Paper*, in line with common practice, the terms merger, acquisition and takeover will be used synonymously.

[2] *British Business*, 13 June 1986, p. 486.

II. TRENDS IN MERGERS

Merger waves are not new in the UK. Figure 1 traces the pattern of mergers in manufacturing since 1900. There are pronounced peaks in the 1920s, the late 1960s and early 1970s. By number, mergers in 1984 and 1985 were fewer and showed no significant increase in the first three-quarters of 1986. These data hardly suggest the existence of merger mania.

The picture by value is, however, somewhat different. In manufacturing the total value of acquisitions in both 1984 and 1985 was in excess of £3,000 million as compared with £1,200 million for the previous peak in 1972. In the second quarter of 1986 alone, the total value of acquisitions in manufacturing was over £5,500 million, reflecting several very large acquisitions. The provisional figure for the third quarter of 1986

Figure 1:

Mergers in UK Manufacturing: 1900–86 (to 3rd Quarter)

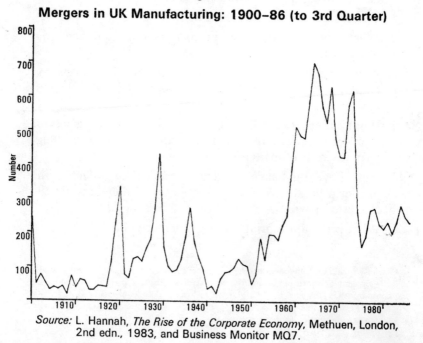

Source: L. Hannah, *The Rise of the Corporate Economy*, Methuen, London, 2nd edn., 1983, and Business Monitor MQ7.

[12]

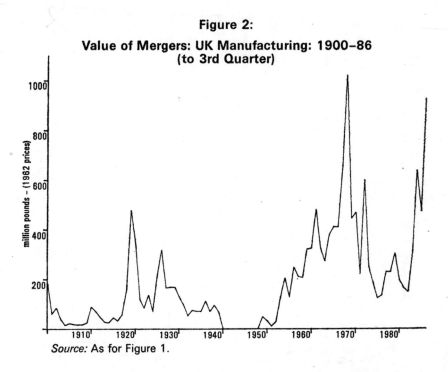

Figure 2:

Value of Mergers: UK Manufacturing: 1900–86
(to 3rd Quarter)

Source: As for Figure 1.

shows a value of £742 million. Such comparisons totally ignore the effects of inflation on the underlying value of the assets. In real terms, after prices have been adjusted to a 1962 base, the position is as shown in Figure 2. Mergers in 1984 and 1985 were clearly not at an historical peak in real terms, although for the first three-quarters of 1986 they were substantially higher, approaching the value for the whole of 1968.

These figures are derived from different data sources and are not strictly comparable.[1] A more consistent series, which includes other industrial and commercial acquisitions, excluding financial companies, is available from 1969. Figure 3 provides the details by number: 1972 and 1973 dominate the period and although in money terms the value of acquisitions at over £7,000 million in 1985 is some three times higher than for 1972, when adjusted for inflation the 1985 figure in real terms is still a little lower than in 1972 (Figure 4). The chart

[1] There are major breaks in comparability in 1919, 1938 and 1968. For a discussion, Leslie Hannah, *The Rise of the Corporate Economy*, Methuen, London, 2nd edn., 1983.

[13]

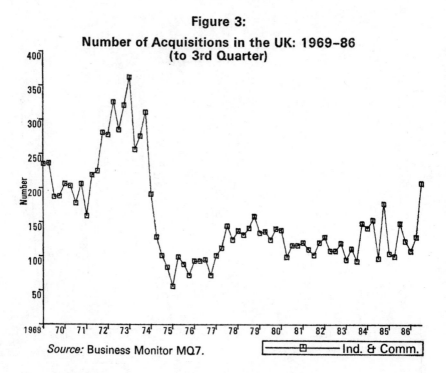

Figure 3:

**Number of Acquisitions in the UK: 1969–86
(to 3rd Quarter)**

Source: Business Monitor MQ7.

Ind. & Comm.

clearly shows the high peak in value terms in the second quarter of 1986. The total value of acquisitions in the second quarter of 1986 was over £6,000 million in current prices, almost as high as that for the whole of 1985.

Trend to large-scale mergers

The conclusion from these figures is that there is nothing unusual about the amount of merger activity in the current period. But there are a number of differences with earlier periods which should be emphasised. First, the average size of acquisition has been much larger in real terms since 1984 than in the early 1970s. Measured in 1962 prices, the average size of acquisition rose from under £1 million in 1972 to over £2 million in 1985 and to almost £4 million in the first three-quarters of 1986. Second, in 1985 and 1986 it was a common occurrence for hostile bids[1] to be made for large companies

[1] A hostile bid is one which is unwelcome and which the victim's management seeks to prevent.

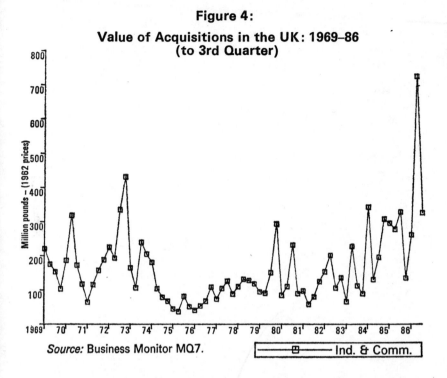

Figure 4:

**Value of Acquisitions in the UK: 1969–86
(to 3rd Quarter)**

Source: Business Monitor MQ7.

where the unwilling target has also sometimes been the subject of more than one bid. Table 1 lists the major bids during 1985-86 and shows that in most cases the victim's managers were unwilling partners. These contests have frequently been acrimonious and costly—an aspect which will be examined below.

The existence of large bids is not, of course, unusual. In 1968, for example, the list included Boots/Timothy Whites, British Motor Holdings/Leyland, National Provincial/Westminster Bank, Thorn/Radio Rentals, and GEC/English Electric. But many of the large bids in the 1960s and early 1970s were conducted as a mutual exercise in the spirit of 'bigness is best' and as a way of enabling British companies to survive in the global market-place. In the 1980s, the issues raised by, for example, Dixons' bid for Woolworths or Hanson Trust's bid for Imperial are not so much about possible economies from large-scale operation as the ability to manage existing assets more effectively, and to set and achieve the best strategy for the enterprise. Since the central issue has become that of

[15]

TABLE 1

MAJOR UK TAKEOVER BIDS

Bidder	Target	Date	Value £billion	Value 1962 Prices £million
United Biscuits	Imperial	Mar. 1986	2·56	295·2
Guinness	Distillers	Mar. 1986	2·35	271·0
Hanson Trust	Imperial	Mar. 1986	2·32	267·6
Argyll	Distillers	Mar. 1986	2·3	265·3
Elders IXL	Allied-Lyons	Oct. 1985	1·8	253·8
Habitat	BHS	Nov. 1985	1·52	203·0
BAT	Eagle Star	Nov. 1983	0·97	199·1
Dixons	Woolworth	June 1986	1·65	190·1
Grand Metropolitan	Watney Mann	Apr. 1972	0·38	172·3
GEC	Plessey	Dec. 1985	1·2	170·2
Lloyds	Standard Chartered	June 1986	1·22	140·6
BTR	T. Tilling	June 1983	0·66	134·8
BTR	Pilkington	Nov. 1986	1·1	124·1
Imperial	Courage	Aug. 1972	0·26	114·7
BAT	Hambro Life	Dec. 1984	0·66	104·3

Note: Does not include £1·25 billion bid for the Canadian company Hiram-Walker by Allied-Lyons in April 1986.

control of the corporation, it is not surprising that the bid is resisted by the existing management of the sought-after firm.

Traditionally, the attention of students of mergers has been focussed upon the acquisition of independent companies by parent groups. Two other important aspects of transfers of ownership need to be addressed, however. The first is the sale of subsidiaries between parent groups, which might be termed parent-to-parent divestments. The second is management buy-outs, whereby the management of a company, with or without the aid of a financing institution, acquires the business by which they are employed. Consideration of the nature of mergers and acquisitions in these three ways enables a wider set of issues to be examined than is often the case, with important implications for policy.

[16]

TABLE 2
ACQUISITIONS, DIVESTMENTS AND
BUY-OUTS, 1969 TO 1985 AND 1986 (to 3rd Quarter)

Year	Acquisition of Independent Industrial Companies[1]			Sales of Subsids. between Industrial Parent Groups[1]			Management Buy-outs[2]		
	No. Acquired	£m.	Avge. £m.	No.	£m.	Avge. £m.	No.	£m.	Avge. £m.
1969	742	961	1·30	102	100	0·98			
1970	608	954	1·57	179	126	0·7			
1971	620	745	1·20	264	166	0·63			
1972	931	2,337	2·51	272	185	0·68			
1973	951	1,057	1·11	254	247	0·97			
1974	367	459	1·25	137	49	0·36			
1975	200	221	1·11	115	70	0·61			
1976	242	348	1·44	111	100	0·90			
1977	372	730	1·96	109	94	0·86	13		
1978	441	977	2·22	126	163	1·29	23		
1979	414	1,438	3·47	117	186	1·59	52	26	0·50
1980	368	1,265	3·44	101	210	2·08	107	50	0·47
1981	327	882	2·70	125	262	2·10	124	114	0·92
1982	296	1,373	4·64	164	804	4·90	170	265	1·56
1983	302	1,783	5·90	142	436	3·07	205	315	1·54
1984	396	4,253	10·74	170	1,121	6·59	210	255	1·21
1985	339	6,281	18·53	134	793	5·92	229	1,176	5·02
1986/Q3	349	10,000	28·65	93	914	9·83	201	944	4·70

Notes:

[1] *Source: Business Monitor Q M7* (various issues).

[2] M. Wright and J. Coyne, *Management Buy-outs in 1985*, Centre for Management Buy-out Research/Venture Economics, September 1985.

The absolute and relative extent of these types of transfers of ownership for the period from 1969 to the third quarter of 1986 are shown in Table 2. The data for independent companies and parent-to-parent divestments refer to industrial and commercial companies, whereas those for buy-outs are for all types. The series for financial company acquisitions ceased publication in 1978, though the Office of Fair Trading provides an analysis of financial acquisitions falling within its terms of reference.

Acquisition of independent firms clearly accounts for the major proportion of transfers of ownership, both by number and value throughout the period. Parent-to-parent divestments as a proportion of the acquisition of independent companies varies considerably, being most important in 1975 and 1982. Since 1982, 30 per cent of all acquisitions by parent groups have been of subsidiaries of other groups. The extent of sales of subsidiaries between parent groups since 1969 demonstrates that divestments are not simply a function of a recession, but have always been a feature of corporate strategic re-alignment. The development of management buy-outs in the last decade has been remarkable. Indeed, in terms of numbers, buy-outs have exceeded parent-to-parent divestments in every year since 1980 except 1981. Buy-outs have, on average, tended to be smaller in terms of price paid than their counterpart sales of subsidiaries to new parents.

Growth of divestment

The growing importance of divestment in the market-place in acquisitions may be seen from a combination of the buy-out and parent-to-parent divestment figures. Estimates suggest that about 70 per cent of buy-outs are divestments from parental groups.[1] On this basis, an adjustment of the figures in Table 2 shows that in 1985 some 46 per cent of all ownership changes were divestments (21·2 per cent by value) compared with 36 per cent (17 per cent by value) in 1980.

The average size figures for transfers of ownership mask wide dispersions. In general, although large mergers are small in number, they account for a substantial proportion of total acquisition expenditure. In 1985, for example, only 17·9 per cent of the acquisitions of independent companies were worth £10 million or more, though their total value accounted for 84 per cent of the cost of all independent company acquisitions. For parent-to-parent divestments, 11·9 per cent cost £10 million or more, accounting for 52·9 per cent of the cost of this type of acquisition. For management buy-outs, 8·3 per cent cost over £10 million, some 80 per cent of the value of

---

[1] The remainder includes mainly buy-outs on retirement and from receivership.

[18]

TABLE 3

INTERNATIONAL ASPECTS OF MERGERS, 1969 TO 1985
AND 1986 (1st Quarter)

Year	Inward Acquisition			Outward Acquisition		
	No. Acqd.	£m.	Average £m.	No. Acqd.	£m.	Average £m.
1969	27	58	2·15	43	29	0·67
1970	23	57	2·48	52	106	2·04
1971	21	33	1·57	62	73	1·18
1972	18	41	2·28	85	90	1·06
1973	8	58	7·25	88	179	2·03
1974	9	185	20·56	53	121	2·28
1975	9	54	6·00	18	41	2·28
1976	10	73	7·30	17	65	3·82
1977	12	80	6·67	18	143	7·94
1978	13	39	3·00	30	350	11·67
1979	6	47	7·83	63	345	5·48
1980	23	170	7·39	51	941	18·45
1981	75	493	6·57	150	726	4·84
1982	29	230	7·93	95	770	8·11
1983	24	198	8·25	71	367	5·17
1984	28	512	18·29	82	821	10·01
1985	21	224	10·67	65	932	14·34
1986/Q1	6	49	8·17	6	274	45·67

Source: Business Monitor MQ7 (various issues).

all buy-outs in 1985. One deal alone (Mardon Packaging) was worth £273 million.

The impact of large acquisitions on the number of independent companies in the UK is quite profound. Of the top 200 companies, ranked by profitability in 1971-72, some 45 ceased to be independent companies by 1984. Between 1982 and 1986, 137 of the top 1,000 quoted companies in the UK in terms of market value in 1982 were acquired or had merged with other companies, indicating the extent to which large companies have been vulnerable to takeovers. Such a feature is also true of earlier merger waves.

Acquisition behaviour has also an international dimension,

[19]

TABLE 4

ACQUISITIONS AND MERGERS AMONGST
BUILDING SOCIETIES, 1955 TO 1985

Period	Acquisitions (Engagements Transferred)	Mergers (Unions)	No. of Societies at start of Period
1955–69	69	7	n.a.
1960–64	82	15	726
1965–69	98	18	n.a.
1970–74	89	4	481
1975–79	108	8	382
1980–84	82	3	273
1985	19	1	167

Source: BSA Fact Book, BSA Statistics.

which may be divided into inward and outward purchases.[1] The figures are provided in Table 3. Over the period 1969-85 the extent of both these kinds of activity fluctuated from year to year in number and in value. Compared with the total figures shown in Table 2, inward acquisition generally accounts for less than 5 per cent of the number and less than 10 per cent of value, with the average size of acquisition being rather larger than foreign acquisitions by domestic firms.

Merger trends in the building societies

The building society sector is outside the scope of many of the published figures on mergers but offers an interesting illustration of the trends. The industry is characterised by increasing concentration since the beginning of the century, and the number of societies has been reduced from 2,286 in 1900 to 167 at the end of 1985. As Table 4 shows, this process has continued strongly since the mid-1950s, so that the number of societies at the end of 1985 was less than a quarter of the number in 1960.

Most mergers have been the takeover of small societies by larger ones to exploit economies of scale, to provide a wider

[1] Inward acquisition concerns the purchase of UK companies by foreign firms whereas outward acquisition is the purchase of foreign companies by UK firms.

geographical branch network and a broader range of services. The impact of mergers on the concentration ratio has been marked. The percentage of assets accounted for by the top five societies has increased from 50·1 per cent in 1970 to 56·8 per cent in 1985 and that of the top 20 from 77·4 to 89·4 per cent over the same period.

The Chief Registrar of Friendly Societies has been particularly active in encouraging mergers between smaller societies and larger ones as a precaution where the margin between net reserves and lending of the smaller societies became too narrow. The changes contained in the new Building Societies Act and its consequences, together with the developments occurring elsewhere in the financial services sector, may be expected to have a further profound effect on the number of societies and the nature of competition. Moreover, the ability of societies to diversify, and to become limited liability companies, as contained in the new Act, is likely to have a significant impact upon the extent of mergers between what have hitherto been considered totally separate institutions within the financial services sector.[1]

---

[1] For a review of the building societies industry, M. Wright, T. Watkins, C. Price and J. Hughes, *The Future of the Building Societies*, Economist Special Publications, No. 1057, July 1986. For an analysis of trends in personal financial services, R. L. Carter, B. Chiplin and M. K. Lewis, *Personal Financial Markets*, Philip Allan, Oxford, 1986.

III. MERGERS AND THE FIRM

Acquisition is generally seen as part of the process of growth of the firm, but it may also be a means of rationalising the structure of declining industries.[1] Growth can be achieved either through investment in additional new or second-hand plant and equipment by the firm (internal growth) or by the acquisition of existing going-concerns (external growth). As Edith Penrose has noted,[2] a firm will choose between internal and external growth according to which is the most profitable. If expansion is considered profitable, regardless of any change in the position of other producers, or in the distribution of the ownership of existing assets, the firm will expand through acquisition only if it is cheaper than internal growth. In that case a crucial issue is why some companies become 'cheap' purchases for expanding firms. If, however, the firm is seeking to change the pattern of existing producers (for example, to bring about a reduction in competition) or change the distribution of control over existing assets (such as patents, control of raw materials, management expertise, etc.), then acquisition may be the only means of achieving these objectives.

An acquisition is an act of mutual exchange whereby the current owners of a company accept cash, securities, or some combination in return for their shares in the existing company. An immediate point is that voluntary mutual exchange only takes place if it is in the perceived interests of both parties and implies a difference in valuation between the buyer and the seller. Thus, the activity of buying and selling a company is, in principle, no different from any other transaction.[3] To the acquirer the purchase is an act of investment which may be evaluated in the same way as any other investment. The acquirer gains the additional cash flows and benefits stemming

---

[1] For an analysis of the causes of mergers in a UK context, K. D. George and A. Silberston, 'The Causes and Effects of Mergers', *Scottish Journal of Political Economy*, 1975, pp. 179-93.

[2] E. T. Penrose, *The Theory of the Growth of the Firm*, Basil Blackwell, Oxford, 1966.

[3] Michael Gort, 'An Economic Disturbance Theory of Mergers', *Quarterly Journal of Economics*, November 1969.

from control in return for the transaction and purchase costs of the acquisition. The selling shareholders gain the difference between the price paid for the shares by the bidder and the expected returns under existing management as measured by the stock market. As with any other exchange, although there must be mutual benefits, the distribution of the gains depends on the state of competition in the market for acquisitions; the more competitive the market the larger the proportion that will accrue to the shareholders of the firm taken over.

Motives for merger

The above discussion has highlighted the possibility of acquisition occurring when gains are available, but has not examined the source of these gains or the motives of the bidder. There are two broad approaches to the question: the first sees firms as value maximisers, whilst the second refers to the managerial motives of the bidding firm. '

In the value-maximising approach the bidder makes a decision on the basis of the economic return to the investment, and the expected economic gain must, therefore, be positive for the bid to be undertaken. The source of the gain derives from a number of possibilities:

(i) *Efficiency* may be increased where the bidder can use the assets of the victim more effectively than its present management because of economies of scale or economies in transaction costs.[1] Such gains may also accrue through synergy, where the combining of activities results in cost savings or higher output for the same input—also known as the '2 + 2 = 5' effect, implying that the expected net cash flow of the combined unit is larger than the sum of the constituent parts as separate entities.

(ii) *Financial gains* may be achieved by redeploying excess cash, or reducing risk through diversification, so that the financial performance and stability of the new enterprise is improved.

---

[1] To the individual firm these benefits may derive from pecuniary economies (the ability to obtain a reduction in input prices through the increased size of the enterprise). Such pecuniary economies simply represent a transfer of wealth from input suppliers to the output producer and hence do not reflect real resource savings to society as a whole.

[23]

(iii) *Information asymmetries* could mean that the bidder has information about the target firm, obtained, for example, through specific company research not available to other market participants and hence not reflected in the current market price of the shares. If so, the acquirer is able to obtain assets at a discount from their true value, as is perhaps best illustrated by the example of firms such as Hanson Trust which have realised that the resale value of separate parts of the enterprise may amount to as much, if not more, than the stock market value of the whole. Thus Hanson Trust was able to recoup almost two-thirds of the costs of acquiring the Imperial Group through subsequent sales (including Courage), whilst retaining subsidiaries which accounted for 55 per cent of Imperial's profits.

(iv) *Increased market power*—enabling a rise in price relative to cost.

Much merger activity in the late 1960s and early 1970s seems to have been motivated by the view that economies of scale (and to some extent of scope) would be achieved, with a consequent improvement in the total performance of the UK economy. There is little evidence that mergers in this period resulted in substantial economies of scale. Frequently, acquisitions continued to be run as independent entities for reasons which will be discussed in Section IV. Technological change has also altered the appropriate configuration of assets required to obtain technological economies of scale and scope across a wide spectrum of industries.

There is also evidence to suggest[1] that the natural monopoly element in the structure of certain industries has been eroded by technological change. Hence economic efficiency may be obtained by having more than one firm in sectors previously regarded as able to support only one.

Technological change may also affect the rationale for economies of scope so that products previously produced jointly may henceforth be more efficiently produced in separate organisations. This feature may particularly apply, for example, as a result of technological change in the personal financial services

---

[1] For a review, B. Chiplin and M. Wright, 'Competition Policy and State Enterprises in the UK', *Antitrust Bulletin*, Winter 1982.

sector.[1] Where the market desires products to be offered to-gether—for instance, in a full home-purchase service covering estate agency, legal requirements and financial provision—joint ventures between different firms may be preferable to supply by a single firm.

Managerial motives relate to the alternative theories of the firm which see the divorce between ownership and control as enabling the management to pursue their own objectives, such as growth or sales maximisation.[2] Acquisitions of this type would have no economic gain to be distributed amongst the owners and hence any gains to the target firm's shareholders must be at the expense of shareholders in the bidding firm.[3]

[1] Brian Chiplin, 'The Impact of Technological Change', in R. L. Carter, B. Chiplin and M. K. Lewis, op. cit.

[2] For example, W. J. Baumol, Business Behaviour, Value and Growth, Macmillan, New York, 1967; Robin Marris, The Economic Theory of Managerial Capitalism, Macmillan, London, 1964; and D. C. Mueller, 'A Theory of Conglomerate Mergers', Quarterly Journal of Economics, 1969.

[3] For example, Paul Halpern, 'Corporate Acquisitions: A Theory of Special Cases?', Journal of Finance, May 1983, pp. 297-317. Managers do gain from an an improvement in their utility, but such gains are not available for distribution.

IV. THE MARKET FOR CORPORATE CONTROL

Whatever the motive for acquisition, the transaction takes place within the market for corporate control. Corporate control is generally taken to be the right to determine the management of corporate resources, for example, the right to hire, fire and set the compensation of top-level management.[1] Takeovers can, therefore, be seen as part of the managerial labour market and, in the market for corporate control, alternative management teams compete for these rights.

The stock market is seen as performing two functions: it allocates capital resources to their most profitable use and ensures that existing assets are most profitably used. An important question (discussed below) is whether it actually performs these tasks well. In principle, companies with poor records of profitability and low expectations of future performance will have low share prices which will increase the difficulty of raising new funds. However, given the importance of self-finance, such control may operate only intermittently and the threat of takeover is seen as a more important disciplinary device. In other words, managements which do not seek to maximise shareholder welfare, or which operate inefficiently, will be penalised by a takeover bid. If the market for corporate control worked perfectly, and transaction costs were zero, no management would survive that did not maximise the wealth of shareholders. The discipline on managerially controlled firms is, therefore, seen as taking place through this market. Such a function of takeovers was recognised by Robin Marris and Henry Manne.[2]

Threat of takeover the key factor

The discipline imposed by the market for corporate control is regarded by many as central to the functioning of a private

[1] E. F. Fama and M. C. Jensen, 'Separation of Ownership and Control', *Journal of Law and Economics*, June 1983.

[2] R. Marris, *The Economic Theory of Managerial Capitalism*, op. cit., and H. Manne, 'Mergers and the Market for Corporate Control', *Journal of Political Economy*, Vol. 73, April 1965.

enterprise economy. Its operation in practice is, therefore, of great significance, and the findings on this topic will be discussed in some detail later (pp. 65-76). It is important to note that it is the *threat* of takeover rather than the acquisition itself which is seen as the motivating factor. Existing management is presumed to take steps, by increasing efficiency and profitability, to prevent a takeover.

Two recent developments are significant here: first, the growth in large mergers and, second, developments in financing arrangements which have made it somewhat easier for smaller firms to acquire larger ones. One implication is that all except the very largest companies are now susceptible to a bid. A recent feature in the *Sunday Times*[1] claimed that British Telecom, BP, Shell and Unilever were probably the only companies likely to be immune from the process. Indeed, several large companies seem to be taking the threat seriously and adjusting their basic strategies accordingly.[2] Companies are also investigating or introducing practices which make the takeover business more difficult, without necessarily leading to an improvement in the use of economic resources. The types of practice and the financing arrangements involved in such bids are discussed later (Section V).

Theoretical deficiencies

As well as practical problems, such as the size of transaction costs, there are also some theoretical deficiencies in the market for corporate control as a disciplinary device. Grossman and Hart provide a cogent analysis of one major problem,[3] that in a company with dispersed share ownership each individual shareholder knows that his or her decision will not affect the outcome of the bid. The small shareholder will thus have an incentive to hold on to his shares in anticipation of a rise in

[1] John Whitmore, 'Takeovers: Who'll Fall Next?', *Sunday Times*, 6 July 1986, p. 57.

[2] P&O is a good example: following a successful defence against a takeover bid from Trafalgar House in 1984, it has succeeded in raising its market capitalisation from £300 million to £1·6 billion over two years. This change included a £750 million merger with Sterling Guarantee Trust in 1984. In December 1986, P&O completed an agreed bid with European Ferries following clearance from the Monopolies Commission. For a discussion, 'Sterling Qualities on the Crest of a Wave', *Sunday Times*, 7 December 1986, p. 61.

[3] S. Grossman and O. Hart, 'Takeover Bids, the Free Rider Problem, and the Theory of the Corporation', *Bell Journal of Economics*, Spring 1980, pp. 42-64.

their price associated with the expected improved post-merger performance of the company. This improved performance has the characteristics of a 'public good' in that it is available to all shareholders and the small shareholders of the target company can seek to enjoy a 'free ride' on the potential gains. If small shareholders in the target company expect the bid to succeed they will have no incentive to sell their shares at a price which would yield the bidder a profit, particularly after taking into account the transaction costs. Consequently, the effectiveness of the market for corporate control in disciplining management is much reduced.

A number of factors make the problem less severe in practice, including differences in valuation between the bidder and the target shareholders and the ability to operate some form of exclusionary device such as compulsory acquisition of minority shareholders or oppression of minority interests. In addition, there are usually several large institutional shareholders in any publicly quoted company of reasonable size. Each of these, therefore, has to make a decision and cannot 'free ride'. Section V examines the rules of the game and how they operate in the market for corporate control.

V. THE RULES OF THE GAME

The regulation of mergers in the UK involves both competition policy and self-regulation through the Panel on Mergers and Takeovers of the Stock Exchange. This section will also consider issues relating to insider dealing, taxation and defences against takeover.

Merger policy

The provision to examine mergers as part of competition policy was first introduced in the 1965 Monopolies and Mergers Act and has been continued under the 1973 Fair Trading Act.[1] Under the legislation an investigation of a merger is conducted by the Monopolies and Mergers Commission (MMC) following a reference by the Secretary of State who is advised by the Director General of Fair Trading. Thus, only the Secretary of State may actually make a reference, and to do so mergers must satisfy one of two criteria—a market share test or an assets test. The minimum market share is fixed at 25 per cent under the Fair Trading Act. The assets threshold was raised to £30 million in July 1984. Parties to an acquisition or merger are not required to notify the authorities of their proposals,[2] but the Director General of Fair Trading has a duty to keep himself informed of all mergers possibly qualifying for reference. Before the Director General of Fair Trading advises the Secretary of State he consults an inter-departmental Mergers Panel.

In July 1984, the then Secretary of State, Mr Norman Tebbit, made an important policy statement in which he said:

'I regard mergers policy as an important part of the government's general policy of promoting competition within the economy in the interests of the customer and of efficiency and hence of

---

[1] For a review of the operation of policy up to 1975, Brian Chiplin, *Acquisitions and Mergers: Government Policy in Europe*, Wilton House/Financial Times, London, 1975.

[2] In practice most do advise the Office of Fair Trading of their intentions and seek preliminary guidance.

growth and jobs. Accordingly my policy has been and will continue to be to make references primarily on competition grounds'.[1]

In evaluating the competitive situation in individual cases Mr Tebbit said he would have regard to the international context—to the extent of competition in the home market from non-UK sources; and to the competitive position of UK companies in overseas markets. This statement was designed to clarify policy on referrals, and has not been repudiated by any subsequent Minister. But the reference of Elders IXL and Allied-Lyons in December 1985 was made on non-competition grounds (methods of finance), and hence there remains some doubt about how far the intentions are carried out in practice.

The Monopolies and Mergers Commission is required to investigate a reference and report whether the merger concerned operates or may be expected to operate against the public interest. Section 84(1) of the Fair Trading Act specifies the public interest as follows:

'In determining for any purposes to which this section applies whether any particular matter operates, or may be expected to operate, against the public interest, the Commission shall take into account all matters which appear to them in any particular circumstances to be relevant and, among other things, shall have regard to the desirability—

a. of maintaining and promoting effective competition between persons supplying goods and services in the UK;

b. of promoting the interests of consumers, purchasers and other users of goods and services in the UK in respect of the prices charged for them and in respect of their quality and the variety of goods and services supplied;

c. of promoting, through competition, the reduction of costs and the development and use of new techniques and new products, and of facilitating the entry of new competitors into existing markets;

d. of maintaining and promoting the balanced distribution of industry and employment in the UK; and

e. of maintaining and promoting competitive activity in markets outside the UK on the part of producers of goods, and of suppliers of goods and services, in the UK.'

In determining the public interest, therefore, the Com-

---

[1] *British Business*, 13 July 1984, p. 381.

TABLE 5

MERGER REFERRALS TO MONOPOLIES AND MERGERS COMMISSION, 1965 TO 1985

Period	Within Legislation No.	% of all mergers	Referred No.	% of relevant mergers
1965–69	466	10·5	10	2·1
1970–74	579	11·4	19	3·3
1975–79	903	36·5	19	2·1
1980–84	987	38·6	31	3·1
1985	192	38·3	4	2·1

Source: Annual Reports of Director General of Fair Trading.

mission is required to take account of any matters it considers relevant, together with a number of particular issues, including the promotion of competition, consumers' interests, industrial efficiency and innovation, the maintenance of a regional balance in industry and employment, and the promotion of competitive activity by UK companies in export markets. The maximum time allowed for a merger report is six months. If the Commission finds the merger to be against the public interest the Secretary of State still has discretion to allow the merger to proceed.

A benign policy

British policy towards merger is, therefore, essentially benign and carries the presumption that mergers are generally in the public interest.[1] A merger has to be found against the public interest by the Commission in order to prevent it: the party or parties do not have to prove that the merger would be *in* the public interest. The Director General of Fair Trading, Sir Gordon Borrie, has recently suggested that the burden of proof might be reversed, perhaps for mergers above a certain size, as a way of tackling the problem of financial markets taking a short-term view, which could be against the public interest.[2]

[1] There is no presumption that a *referred* merger is or is not against the public interest.

[2] *Financial Times*, 6 December 1986, p. 10. 'Short-termism' is discussed in Section VI, pp. 53-55.

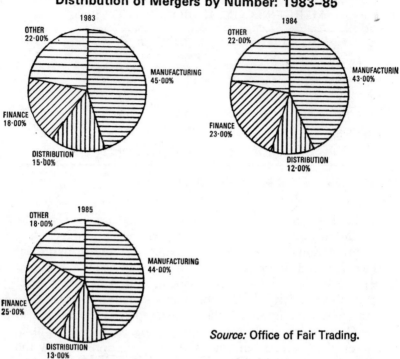

Figure 5:

Distribution of Mergers by Number: 1983–85

1983

OTHER 22·00%

MANUFACTURING 45·00%

FINANCE 18·00%

DISTRIBUTION 15·00%

1984

OTHER 22·00%

MANUFACTURIN 43·00%

FINANCE 23·00%

DISTRIBUTION 12·00%

1985

OTHER 18·00%

MANUFACTURING 44·00%

FINANCE 25·00%

DISTRIBUTION 13·00%

Source: Office of Fair Trading.

Office of Fair Trading and MMC scrutiny

As shown earlier, not all merger activity comes within the scope of the relevant legislation and the number of mergers so doing is given in Table 5. The failure to increase the assets criterion in line with inflation brought an increasing proportion of mergers within the terms of the Act. Had the £30 million assets figure applied from 1980, for example, some 694 rather than 987 mergers would have been eligible for consideration. Between 2 and 3 per cent of relevant mergers have been referred to the MMC for investigation each year. The Tebbit guidelines discussed earlier placed emphasis on the competitive aspects of mergers in the decision to refer or not. Of the references to the MMC since 1965, about one-third have been in the service sector and that proportion has been increasing over time. During the last three years the proportion of eligible mergers in the financial services sector has increased from 18 per cent in 1983 to 25 per cent in 1985 (Figure 5).

[32]

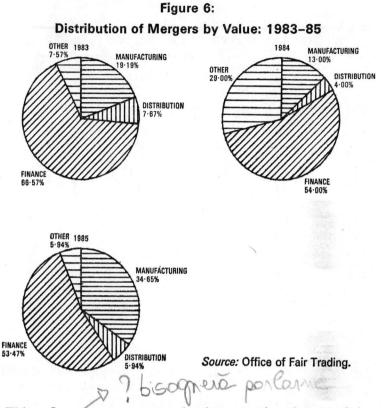

Figure 6:

Distribution of Mergers by Value: 1983–85

OTHER 1983
7·57%
MANUFACTURING
19·19%

DISTRIBUTION
7·67%

FINANCE
66·57%

1984
OTHER
29·00%
MANUFACTURING
13·00%

DISTRIBUTION
4·00%

FINANCE
54·00%

OTHER 1985
5·94%
MANUFACTURING
34·65%

FINANCE
53·47%
DISTRIBUTION
5·94%

Source: Office of Fair Trading.

This reflects to some extent developments in advance of the 'Big Bang' in October 1986. The figures by value (Figure 6) are susceptible to the impact of major mergers in particular sectors and show the proportion by value in financial services falling over the period. Likewise, although the proportion of eligible mergers in manufacturing has been fairly constant, its share in value terms rose substantially in 1985 to 35 per cent.

Merger characteristics and the MMC

Mergers can have horizontal, vertical or diversifying characteristics.[1] The indication from Table 6 is that vertical integration mergers have traditionally accounted for a very small element of the total activity falling within the Act. The relative importance of horizontal and conglomerate mergers has fluctuated

---

[1] For an extensive analysis of diversification, A. W. Goudie and G. Meeks, 'Diversification by Merger', *Economica*, 1982, pp. 447-59.

[33]

TABLE 6
TYPES OF ACQUISITION/MERGER
WITHIN LEGISLATION, 1970 TO 1985 (PER CENT)

	Horizontal		Vertical		Diversifying	
	by number	by value	by number	by value	by number	by value
1970–74	73	65	5	4	23	27
1975	71	77	5	4	24	19
1976	70	66	8	7	22	27
1977	64	57	11	11	25	32
1978	53	67	13	10	34	23
1979	51	68	7	4	42	28
1980	65	68	4	1	31	31
1981	62	71	6	2	32	27
1982	65	64	5	4	30	32
1983	71	73	4	1	25	26
1984	63	79	4	1	33	20
1985	58	42	4	4	38	54

Source: Office of Fair Trading.

widely over the last 15 years, with the proportion of horizontal mergers by value at its lowest in 1985, and diversifying mergers correspondingly being at their highest. Horizontal mergers have accounted for the largest proportion of referrals to the MMC over the last 20 years (Table 7), representing 60 per cent of all referrals. Over a quarter of referred mergers have subsequently been abandoned and, of those investigated by the Commission, 38 per cent have been declared to contain features contrary to the public interest. Investigations of vertical mergers are least likely to be found against the public interest, with horizontal mergers being the most troublesome. Table 8 provides a summary of the principal issues involved in the merger reports by the Monopolies Commission since 1983. Obstacles to competition appear to be given significant weight in finding a proposed merger to be against the public interest, but as would be expected under the Section 84 criteria, there are many other factors which receive consideration.[1]

[1] For a discussion of the cases until 1969, J. F. Pickering, 'British Competition Policy on Mergers', *European Community Law Review*, 1980.

TABLE 7

OUTCOME OF MMC INVESTIGATIONS, 1965 TO 1985

Structural Change	Referred	Aban-doned	Public Interest Conclusion Against	Public Interest Conclusion Not Against	% Against
Horizontal	51	10	17	24	41
Vertical	6	1	1	4	20
Conglomerate	26	11	5	10	33
Total	83	22	23	38	38

Source: Review of Monopolies and Merger Policy, Cmnd. 7198, HMSO, 1978 (updated).

The City Takeover Code

The City Code on Takeovers and Mergers is administered by a Panel and applies to public companies. The Code is not backed by legislation but by the understanding that if not observed the facilities of the securities markets in the UK will be withdrawn.[1] The latest version has been in operation since April 1985.

The Code consists of two parts: a set of general principles; and a series of rules. The general principles largely require equality of treatment between shareholders, and that rights of control should be exercised in good faith. The rules cover a substantial number of issues relating to the need for secrecy, the timing of various stages in the acquisition process, the contents of the offer document, and several requirements in connection with the necessity for formal offers to be made.

The provisions of the Code prevent undesirable partial bids where minority shareholders are likely to be only weakly protected by their legal rights. However, the 1948 Companies

---

[1] On 5 December 1986, the Court of Appeal ruled that decisions of the Takeover Panel may be reviewed by the courts in certain circumstances. Such a judgement runs counter to the non-statutory framework of the City's self-regulation. The Master of the Rolls said that the courts should generally allow panel decisions to take their course and only intervene 'in retrospect' by making declarations enabling the panel not to repeat any error and relieving individuals of the disciplinary consequences of any erroneous finding by the panel in a breach of the City takeover code. (*Financial Times*, 6 December 1986.) The precise implications of this decision remain to be seen, but the Court did not feel that such a legal process could be used as a defence against takeover.

[cont'd on p. 39]

TABLE 8

MONOPOLIES COMMISSION MERGER REPORTS, 1983–86

Case	Year	Finding	Benefits	Detriments
The Enterprise of Alan J. Lewis and Illingworth Morris	1983	Not against	Helps remove uncertainty over I.M.'s future.	
A. Alfred Taubman and Sotheby Parke Bernet Group	1983	Not against		
London Brick and Ibstock Johnsen	1983	Not against	Some benefits from more efficient provision of plant and machinery, research and development, use of transport facilities, use of London Brick's landfill services, and in purchasing of goods and services, but not likely to be substantial. Some overseas benefits, especially brickmaking in the USA.	
Pleasurama and Trident TV and Grand Metropolitan	1983	Against (5:1)		Majority—further increase in market concentration would adversely effect competition. Enhanced barriers to entry through reinforcement of regulatory system favouring existing operators.
Trafalgar House and Peninsular and Oriental Steam Navigation Co.	1984	Not against	Longer-term benefits internationally in construction. Profitability could increase but MMC unsure of likelihood.	P and O's fear of too high debt/equity ratio unfounded.

TABLE 8

MONOPOLIES COMMISSION MERGER REPORTS, 1983–86 *(contd.)*

Case	Year	Finding	Benefits	Detriments
Hepworth Ceramic Holdings and Steetley	1984	Against	Rationalisation of refractories, but these could be achieved without merger and do not outweigh detriments.	Adverse effect on competition in supply of refractories; likely increase in imports.
Guest Keen and Nettlefolds and AE	1984	Against	Rationalisation of R+D and distribution businesses, but not dependent on merger.	Loss of competition in supply of plain bearings and cylinder liners—adverse effects on imports, employment and value added.
The Dee Corporation and Booker McConnell	1985	Not against (4:1)	Majority—Dee strengthened as competitor to largest multiples; better terms from suppliers through greater power—passed on to consumers; cost savings from single head office.	Slight possibility of Dee changing prices to weaken smaller retailers; slight adverse effect on employment.
British Electric Traction Co. and Initial	1985	Not against	Cost savings; long-term increases in employment; enhanced ability to offer services to NHS.	Prima facie decrease in competition but BET acquiring full control would not significantly increase existing influence.
Birmingham Post and Mail Holdings and Yattendon Investment Trust	1985	Not against	Financial improvement may help these newspapers to compete better with other newspapers and safeguard employment.	
United Newspapers and Fleet Holdings	1985	Not against		

TABLE 8

MONOPOLIES COMMISSION MERGER REPORTS, 1983–86 *(contd.)*

Case	Year	Finding	Benefits	Detriments
Scottish and Newcastle Breweries and Matthew Brown	1985	Not against		Closure of breweries not totally secure but irrespective of merger; some loss of employment.
British Telecom and Mitel Corporation	1986	Against (4:1)	Major international presence for BT, but outcome not certain.	Adverse effects on competition between suppliers of telecommunications equipment and distributors. Reinforces BT's dominance of PABX as involves control of vertically integrated manufacture.
BET and SGB Group	1986	Not against	Possible gains in efficiency and ability to get more overseas business.	
General Electric and Plessey	1986	Against (5:1)	Rationalisation of System X; possible long-term benefits but sceptical because of problems in establishing direct link between size and performance.	Adverse effects on supply of transmission equipment, traffic signalling; loss of competition in supply of electronic defence equipment; loss of competitive R+D.
Elders IXL and Allied-Lyons	1986	Not against	Competition may be increased through more aggressive management by Elders.	Possible adverse effect if Elders sell food division of Allied. High leveraging not cause for concern in this case.
Norton Opax and McCorquodale	1986	Not against	Possible overseas growth; net benefits from rationalisation.	Any problems from increased concentration would be matched by countervailing power of banks; entry barriers low in lotteries.

Act included a provision for an acquirer to purchase compulsorily the shares of a dissenting minority. As a general rule, if the acquirer receives acceptances from the holders of not less than 90 per cent (by value) of the shares to which the offer relates, the offeror is entitled to acquire the remaining shares on the same terms as were accepted by the majority. It was argued earlier that because of the public-good aspects, small shareholders may seek to 'free ride' on a takeover bid and hence frustrate the operation of the market for corporate control. As Yarrow points out:

'... UK company law and the City Code on Mergers and Takeovers combine to produce an approximately efficient solution to public good problems connected with takeovers. Compulsory acquisition rights provide the necessary exclusion device when opportunities for oppressive behaviour towards minorities is limited, while the rules of the Code prevent the occurrence of undesirable partial bids in cases where minority shareholders are likely to be only weakly protected by their legal rights. Thus the incentives towards efficient management resulting from the existence of the takeover threat will not be impaired by free-riding strategies, and there is no conflict between policy measures designed to strengthen the position of minorities and to preserve the effectiveness of the takeover mechanism.'[1]

The Takeover Panel introduced amended rules in March 1986 to control the type of advertising which can be used in bid cases.[2] Its action followed a series of advertisements in the Hanson Trust/United Biscuits/Imperial and Argyll/Guinness/ Distillers contested bids. From 7 April 1986, all advertisements in newspapers and on radio and television which do not fall into a number of exempt categories (such as product or corporate image advertising, notices required by the Stock Exchange, etc.) have been banned. Such a ban ignores the role of advertising in providing information to shareholders. Further, it is not clear why 'persuasive' advertising should be regarded as necessarily bad in this context and not in others.

Insider dealing

Insider dealing has been a criminal offence since June 1980. The general principle is that an individual may not deal in

---

[1] G. K. Yarrow, 'Shareholder Protection, Compulsory Acquisition and the Efficiency of the Takeover Process', *Journal of Industrial Economics*, September 1985, pp. 3-16.

[2] For example, *Financial Times*, 27 March 1986, p. 1.

securities on a recognised stock exchange or 'over the counter', if he is in possession of inside information obtained directly or indirectly from another person. The rules of the Takeover Code state that persons privy to price-sensitive information may not deal in the shares. Takeovers provide an excellent opportunity for those with inside knowledge to obtain significant financial rewards. In a study of 194 mergers in the United States covering the period 1974-78, Keown and Pinkerton[1] found abnormal increases in price, relative to the index, around 25 days prior to the merger announcement date and this rise in price was accompanied by a significant increase in trading volume. Their evidence is consistent with the existence of trading based on inside information. Thus they found that market reaction to intended mergers occurs before the first public announcement. Indeed,

> 'the findings show what appears to be common knowledge on the street: impending merger announcements are poorly held secrets, and trading on this non-public information abounds'.

For the UK, a recent analysis of 1985 by *Acquisitions Monthly*[2] showed similar sharp rises in the prices of target companies in advance of the official bid announcement. Of 100 bids studied, the average rise in price was 54 per cent during the six months before the announcement, 39 per cent during the month before and 25 per cent on the day before. Since 1980 the Stock Exchange has referred 93 cases of insider dealing to the Department of Trade and Industry of which five have resulted in prosecutions and three in convictions.

In November 1986 two major cases of insider trading became public, one on each side of the Atlantic. These have prompted widespread investigations of the practice by the authorities in both the UK and the USA. In New York, Mr Dennis Levine, an employee of the investment bank Drexel Burnham Lambert, revealed that he had supplied inside information to Mr Ivan Boesky (a major figure in facilitating takeovers in the USA) in return for 5 per cent of the profits made from the information. Consequently Mr Boesky agreed to pay $100 million in penalties to the Securities and Exchange Commission and

---

[1] A. J. Keown and J. M. Pinkerton, 'Merger Announcements and Insider Trading Activity: An Empirical Investigation', *Journal of Finance*, September 1981, pp. 855-69.

[2] *Sunday Times*, 9 March 1986, pp. 58-59, and *Acquisitions Monthly*, March 1986.

accepted a lifetime ban on securities dealing in America. In London, Mr Geoffrey Collier, a director of Morgan Grenfell Securities, admitted to buying 50,000 shares in AE through his Cayman Island nominee company on which he stood to make around £15,000. The purchase was made before the Hollis Group, advised by Morgan Grenfell, publicly announced a takeover bid for AE.[1] In December 1986 a DTI investigation started into the movements of the Guinness share price during the contest with Argyll Group for control of Distillers. One aspect of the investigation is the extent to which Guinness's share price was manipulated during the acquisition. The investigation has led to the resignation of the Chairman, Finance Director and two non-executive directors of Guinness; resignations of senior members of advising banks and other companies; potential legal action; and a review by the Bank of England of the operation of Morgan Grenfell, the merchant bank involved.[2]

Arguments for insider trading . . .

Henry Manne has argued[3] that existing shareholders selling to insiders would have sold at the agreed price to anyone and hence have suffered no harm (a so-called 'victimless crime'). It might also be argued that transactions by insiders provide a valuable signal to the market which leads to a change in the share price earlier than would otherwise have occurred. Thus, such trading provides valuable new information to the market and prevents transactions taking place at the 'wrong' price. As Anthony Harris has stated:

'Inside information on companies is more reliable than even the most brilliant study of racing form, and a punter who acts on it is giving information to the market; and there was a time when insider dealings were regarded as equally worthy of their profits. The victims, after all, were the market-makers; . . . Indeed, in one sense the insider dealer was a general benefactor; for whereas ordinary racing punters lose potential gains when odds are shortened, ordinary ignorant investors gain when prices are marked up'.[4]

[1] For a discussion of both cases, e.g., *The Economist*, 22-28 November 1986, pp. 81-2.

[2] For example, *Financial Times*, 21 January 1987, p. 1.

[3] 'Defence of Insider Trading', *Harvard Business Review*, Vol. 44, November/December 1966.

[4] 'Please give us back our rules', *Financial Times*, 6 December 1986.

Manne further argues that the insiders who benefit are usually managers who are obtaining a reward for their services in raising the market value of the firm. Demsetz has also claimed[1] that insider trading, as reflected in large individual and family ownership of shares, provides a more effective and continuously active monitoring mechanism than the takeover.

. . . and against

Such arguments in favour of insider trading have little credence when applied to transactions through nominees or when undertaken on their own behalf by employees of financial intermediaries who have access to privileged information. Such transactions do not provide the same signal to the market as when they are undertaken by known 'insiders'. The literature on insider trading (predominantly American) generally defines insiders as individuals who are officers, directors and owners of 10 per cent or more of any equity class of securities as required by the Securities and Exchange Act of 1934. As a recent study of the issue has stated:

'Insiders' abnormal profits do not appear to be especially large. However, insider trading is regulated by the Securities and Exchange Act of 1934. Insiders can be sued for violating their fiduciary responsibilities to their shareholders if they trade on material non-public information prior to the public announcement of the information. Consequently, insiders would not be expected to trade for their own account immediately prior to highly profitable but also publicised corporate events such as mergers and tender offers'.[2]

Hence, arguments about insider trading have to distinguish carefully between the types of 'insiders' involved. As employee share-ownership becomes more widespread the activities of insiders who are employees becomes more significant. However, dealing by 'insiders' of the type exemplified by the Boesky and Collier affairs can have little justification. The problem arises in actually detecting the offenders and taking the appropriate action. As *The Economist* argued:

'The legal argument for treading softly with insider trading is that it is hard to define and police. Is someone who picks up a

[1] Harold Demsetz, 'Corporate Control, Insider Trading and Rates of Return', *American Economic Review Papers and Proceedings*, May 1986, pp. 313-16.

[2] H. N. Seyhun, 'Insiders' Profits, Costs of Trading, and Market Efficiency', *Journal of Financial Economics*, Vol. 16, 1986, pp. 189-212.

rumour that A will bid for B guilty, even if he only buys for somebody else's trust? What if he hears the rumour at work, which happens to be the bank advising A? What if he just repeats the rumour at his golf club? Jail any share-buying barman? . . . Every case will vary in its fine lines and grey areas and diplomatic nuance—so, say cautious lawyers, don't make an ass of the law by asking it to do too much'.[1]

In both Britain and America, however, concern amongst the regulatory authorities is such that strong attempts are being made to deal with the difficult problems involved. In the UK, Mr Paul Channon, the Secretary of State for Trade and Industry, introduced new laws to facilitate investigations into insider dealing with effect from midnight on 14 November 1986. These new laws were brought into operation almost two months ahead of their scheduled introduction, and will allow inspectors appointed by the Trade and Industry Secretary to examine on oath any person whom he considers may have relevant information, and to compel witnesses to answer questions under threat of punishment for contempt of court. The inspectors will also have the power to compel the production of documents.[2] Insider dealing appears a major element in takeover bids and clearly something which both the City and the Government are keen to control. How effective their attempts will be remains to be seen.

The long-run success of suppliers of financial services rests on trust, safety and reputation.[3] Most successful financial institutions have established their credentials over a long period, but a few examples of errant behaviour can undo the work of centuries. There is, therefore, a considerable incentive for institutions to provide effective policing of their activities. The repercussions of the 'Guinness Affair' with the resignation of several directors in both the company itself and its advisers, have shown the potential high costs involved in breaking both the letter and the spirit of the current law.

[1] 'Insider Trading', The Economist, 22-28 November 1986, p. 15.
[2] Financial Times, 15 November 1986.
[3] For an extended discussion, M. K. Lewis and B. Chiplin, 'Characteristics of Markets for Personal Financial Services', in R. L. Carter, B. Chiplin and M. K. Lewis (eds.), op. cit.

Taxation and related issues

An important element in the takeover process is the nature of the taxation régime, which may create distortions such as to provoke a takeover even if the taken-over resources would be used less efficiently by the acquiring company.[1] An acquisition generally has taxation implications for both the acquired and acquiring companies and their shareholders.[2] Before the 1984 Finance Act, profits or losses and chargeable gains to companies were apportioned to two notional accounting periods, one before and one after the date of acquisition. Group taxation relief, enabling trading losses incurred in one subsidiary to be transferred to another within the group or to the group itself, could be obtained only for that period when the acquired company was part of the group. The 1984 Act continued this method unless an unreasonable or unjust result was produced. Where the acquired company has made losses, it is essential for an acquirer wishing to obtain tax relief to continue the trade of the business and to make it profitable.

Determination of whether the trade has continued may be a contentious issue with the Inland Revenue. For example, an acquirer may simply wish to continue with the profitable parts of an acquisition and close down the remainder. Hence, it could be argued that taxation relief is not possible on the ground that the losses occurred in an area of the trade not carried on by the new owner. There may also be a high degree of risk in trying to make a loss-making acquisition profitable, whilst continuing to satisfy the criterion that the trade has continued. Where profitability cannot be attained it will not be possible to take advantage of carried forward losses. The 1970 Taxes Act introduced provisions to curtail the active market in tax-loss companies that had developed to acquire the tax relief. The provisions meant that relief could be obtained only if a transfer of ownership, or a change in the nature of the trade, did not take place within three years of the losses

[1] For example, L. Lowenstein, 'Management Buy-outs', *Columbia Law Review*, November 1985.

[2] For a comprehensive review of the UK position, T. E. Cooke, *Mergers and Acquisitions*, Basil Blackwell, Oxford, 1986. For the taxation implications of mergers in the USA, Michael Smirlock, Randolph Beatty and Saman Majd, 'Taxes and Mergers: A Survey', Monograph Series in Finance and Economics, Salomon Brothers Center for the Study of Financial Institutions, Graduate School of Business Administration, New York University, No. 3, 1985.

being incurred. Relief could not be obtained where trading activities had become negligible and there was a change of ownership before they had recovered. The acquirer, should it subsequently dispose of the acquisition, will be able to obtain relief from Capital Gains Tax for costs incurred in acquisition and disposal and those incurred in enhancing the company's value in the meantime.

Difficulties may arise where the acquired company has previously benefited from the ability to 'roll over' the gains on the sale of one chargeable asset into the tax costs of new assets acquired—a particular problem where the tax cost of assets acquired is equivalent to the proceeds from the sale of the original asset, as the tax liability may be hidden. Other indirect capital gains tax consequences may arise where the proceeds of the sale of one asset are used to acquire a new asset, as the rule for roll-over relief requires both assets to have been used in trade by the same person.

The shareholders of the acquirer should not experience any taxation consequences arising from a takeover, but there may be important repercussions for those of the acquired company. Essentially the taxation consequences depend on whether or not a disposal of shares or debentures has taken place. If the disposal is deemed to be part of a re-organisation carried out for commercial reasons, exemption from tax may be obtained.

These provisions generally relate to the combination of two or more businesses, though to the extent that the acquired company was previously part of a group the conditions also apply. Divestment or separation of the activities of parts of a group raise other taxation issues.

Divestment

In the UK, company law first allowed for the separation of a company into two or more parts (a demerger) under section 206 of the 1948 Companies Act. The procedure involved the distribution of a dividend *in specie*, derived either from capital reserves or a court-approved reduction in share capital. The only tax penalty would be the stamp duty arising if the shares being distributed were transferred, rather than allotted directly to the holding company's shareholders.[1] The 1965 Finance

---

[1] R. Instone, 'Demergers', *New Law Journal*, 18 December 1980, pp. 1,192-94.

Act, at a time when policy was to encourage mergers, introduced taxation penalties on all dividends including those used
to effect a demerger, and hence introduced a bias against
demerging. Schedule 18 of the 1980 Finance Act, however,
provided for the exemption from taxation of distributions to
shareholders that are used to bring about the demerger of an
existing subsidiary, as long as the parent holds at least 75 per
cent interest in the subsidiary, and certain other conditions
are met. These conditions relate to the necessity to show benefits to the trading activities of the newly independent entity
and include the requirement to obtain clearance from the
Inland Revenue that the operation is not a scheme for the
avoidance of tax.

The general view of tax law commentators[1] is that this
change has not so far had the desired effect of helping to break
up ill-fitting conglomerates, but that it has been more useful
in effecting splits in private companies. The framing of the
legislation is considered restrictive; for example, corporation
tax liabilities may arise on the gains derived from the deemed
disposal of a subsidiary. The Inland Revenue also faces a
dilemma in applying the rules since a balance has to be achieved
between encouraging the use of the legislation and restricting
it so as to minimise the incidence of tax avoidance.

Management buy-outs

Such legal complexity has encouraged companies to opt for
relatively less onerous solutions, such as management buy-outs.
Here, too, serious taxation and other hurdles may have to be
negotiated. Where a buy-out is done through acquisition of
shares (the preferred route), the newly independent company
will normally take on the past tax history of the entity and all
that it entails. Problems may arise in negotiations with the
vendor, who may be able to use past tax losses to offset profits
elsewhere in the group. The outcome can have substantial
effects upon future cash flows of the bought-out company.

The bought-out company trying to obtain the advantages
of prior years' tax losses will also have to satisfy a number of
criteria originally designed to prevent the purchase and sale
of tax losses. When it becomes independent, the acquired

[1] For example, P. Lawton, 'Demerger: An Assessment', *The Company Lawyer*, Vol.
5, No. 1, 1984, pp. 17-26.

company may trigger a corporation tax liability on notional capital gains made on, say, property transferred to it elsewhere in the group. In the asset purchase route a basic conflict of interest exists between vendor and purchaser since a tax benefit to one is likely to be a tax disadvantage to the other. Such problems should be resolved through negotiation.[1]

Another major problem to be dealt with in management buy-outs concerns giving financial assistance. Originally designed to protect creditors from having the net assets of a company which owed them money being compromised so that other individuals could obtain funds to buy that company, the legislation contained in Sections 151-156 of the 1985 Companies Act concerning buy-outs is a delicate area. As an illustration, assume that a management team, and its venture capital backers, wish to acquire the company for which they work for £1 million. They provide half the purchase price, but the balance comes from an overdraft and a loan secured on the company's assets. The charge being taken over the assets of the company effectively reduces its unencumbered assets available for the benefit of creditors in general. Section 151 prohibits such transactions and hence a charge given to the bank would be invalid and the bank would have, therefore, no security. Under the terms of the legislation it is possible for financial assistance to be given if the directors swear a Statutory Declaration that having acquired the business they consider it will be able to pay debts as they fall due for a period up to 12 months ahead. This Declaration has to be supported by the company's auditors. These provisions do provide some easing of the legislation originally contained in section 54 of the 1948 Companies Act, but it is by no means an easy route to negotiate in practice.

Defences against takeover

Faced with the rise of the hostile takeover bid, it is not surprising that in both the UK and the USA a number of defensive strategies have been devised which increase the costs of a bid, and hence make the firm less attractive to a predator. Many of these strategies have originated in the United States and

---

[1] For further discussion of the taxation implications of management buy-outs, M. Wright, J. Coyne and A. Mills, *Spicer and Pegler's Management Buy-outs*, Woodhead-Faulkner, Cambridge, 1987.

carry exotic names such as 'golden parachute', 'shark repellent', 'poison pill', 'Pac-Man strategy' and 'greenmail'. These devices have been given the generic name of 'fake-outs' which covers all classes of market mechanisms that allow management with little or no ownership interest to fend off unwanted suitors.[1] A brief description of some of the alternatives will give a flavour of the type of defences involved.

A 'golden parachute' is a contractual agreement with management which provides for substantial severance payments to managers who leave the firm following a takeover. A survey of 665 industrial companies in America in 1982 found that 15 per cent provided such 'golden parachutes' to top management.[2]

A 'shark repellent' (also known as a 'porcupine provision') is where shareholders vote to change the corporate charter to discourage takeover bids and provide for super majority voting on mergers and other impediments to unwanted bids.

A 'poison pill' has many variants but essentially involves the issue of convertible securities which may be converted into shares of the company owning it at the time of the conversion, often on favourable terms. The effect is to raise the cost of the acquisition. The term is also applied to the purchase of unwanted assets, particularly at a high price, which make the firm a less attractive target.

A 'Pac-man defence' (named after a computer game) is where the target company itself puts in a bid for the hostile suitor. It came to prominence in the four-way bid in the US involving Bendix, Martin Marietta, United Technologies and Allied Corporation in 1982. Martin Marietta's reaction to an unwelcome bid from Bendix was to make its own offer for Bendix shares.

'Greenmail' involves a potential victim buying back its own shares at a premium from a raider in return for a promise that there will be no attempt at a takeover.

Defence mechanisms and managerial rewards

All these strategies are designed to raise the costs of an acquisition to make the company less attractive to a potential raider.

[1] Mark Hirschey, 'Mergers, Buyouts and Fakeouts', *American Economic Review Papers and Proceedings*, May 1986, pp. 317-22.

[2] A. M. Morrison, 'Those Executive Bail-out Deals', *Fortune*, 13 December 1982, pp. 82-87.

At first sight, therefore, it would appear that such defences operate to inhibit the takeover mechanism and should be discouraged by public policy. They should, however, be seen in the context of the whole market for corporate control and the reward structure of top management. Most of these arrangements are introduced with the agreement of existing shareholders, thus implying that both parties to the exchange—managers and shareholders—expect to benefit. As Knoeber has recently argued,[1] the contract between managers and shareholders is an important source of discipline on managerial behaviour and often the best contract is implicit, with much compensation delayed until the performance of the management can be better evaluated. In this environment golden parachutes and shark repellents reduce the likelihood that a successful bid will allow new owners to remove the management and capture the delayed compensation. They can be viewed as a mechanism adopted by shareholders to ensure managers of their reliability and therefore induce them to accept a contract which makes both parties better off. Hirschey[2] has similarly argued that these defence mechanisms can be seen as part of the market process whereby incumbent management is able to obtain a larger share of the rentals accruing to their firm-specific human capital. They are thus an essential part of the market for managerial talent.

In the UK, the operation of such strategies is restricted by the Takeover Code during the bid period, but many companies are already reviewing the alternatives and introducing provisions in anticipation of a bid to make takeover more difficult. What has been seen, for example, is a company subject to an unwanted bid itself putting in a bid for another company, thus making itself larger and more expensive to acquire. Two recent cases were the £1·25 billion bid by Allied-Lyons for the Canadian Group Hiram-Walker whilst itself the subject of a bid from Elders IXL, and Plessey's consideration of the purchase of the American company DSC Communications whilst the bid for Plessey by GEC had been referred to the Monopolies Commission.[3]

[1] C. R. Knoeber, 'Golden Parachutes, Shark Repellents and Hostile Tender Offers', *American Economic Review*, March 1986, pp. 155-67.

[2] 'Mergers, Buyouts and Fakeouts', *op. cit.*

[3] *The Economist*, 5 April 1986, p. 76, and 'Plessey's Poison Pill', *Sunday Times*, 4 May 1986, p. 57.

Another common defence is to seek a 'white knight', that is, a competing bid from a more welcome suitor, as in the Eagle Star-BAT case where Eagle Star was seeking to prevent its acquisition by Allianz. Similarly, Guinness was seen as a white knight by Distillers faced with a bid from Argyll. The managers may have a number of reasons for viewing their interests as best served by an alternative bidder; shareholders ultimately can choose between the alternatives and are, at least, given the opportunity to assess the rival claims.

In the UK it is also not unknown for the target company to seek to encourage the referral of a bid to the Monopolies Commission for investigation. It has to be remembered that reference is made by the Secretary of State following advice from the Director General of Fair Trading, and a number of companies have engaged in substantial lobbying to try to secure a reference, for example, London Brick before it was taken over by Hanson Trust. The fact that a reference to the Commission may effectively kill the prospects of a merger, primarily because of the delay it entails, leads to a high premium on lobbying.

The cost of takeover bids

Several of the recent large hostile bids in the UK have found public expression in major advertising campaigns which, as mentioned earlier, have now been banned by the City Panel on Takeovers and Mergers. These recent battles have also highlighted the large costs that can be incurred: for example, underwriting, fees to merchant bankers and advertising cost Argyll nearly £50 million in its unsuccessful bid for Distillers, and although Argyll made a profit of around £20 million on selling its Distillers' shares, the net cost remained at around £30 million. John Kay estimates the transactions costs of takeovers in the first six months of 1986 at £600 million.[1] Transactions costs are an essential part of any market exchange, but naturally the higher such costs the lower the amount of trade. It is not true to argue, as Kay does, that they represent expenditure that produces nothing at all of value, for without them there would be no takeover mechanism and no scope to realise economies through merger. From the viewpoint of the

[1] In a paper presented to an Institute of Fiscal Studies Conference on Acquisitions and Mergers, July 1986—'Counting the Cost of Merger Mania', *Sunday Times*, 20 July 1986, p. 61.

public interest it is essential to ensure that these costs do not include any monopoly rents and that the market for these transaction services is competitive. Changes since the 'Big Bang' in October 1986 should lead to a reduction in such costs. The role of merchant banks and other institutions in the acquisition process has also been undergoing something of a transformation in recent months. Thus a number of banks and banking groups have been acquiring strategic shareholdings in companies engaged in bids and also buying individual subsidiaries from groups involved in takeovers. These activities led the Bank of England to issue guidelines on the role of banks in takeovers which, amongst other things, placed an upper limit on exposure in any one such acquisition of 25 per cent of the bank's capital base. Moreover, the DTI investigation into Distillers, noted earlier, may well have general implications for the role of such advisers during takeover bids.

VI. FINANCIAL ASPECTS OF MERGERS

This section considers the role of financial institutions in the merger process, along with the claim that they place undue emphasis on short-term gains at the expense of long-term performance. The question of bond financing with its implications for capital gearing is also analysed.

Institutional shareholdings

One possible solution to the principal-agent problem caused by the divorce between ownership and control in the wake of a dispersion of shareholdings, is to increase the proportion of shares held by institutions. Analysis by Cosh et al.[1] indicates that performance in companies with significant institutional shareholdings is better than where this is not the case, and that post-merger profitability increases for such firms.

It is difficult to argue a priori that this difference in performance should necessarily arise. One problem is that it may be difficult to decide the direction of causality—are firms more profitable because of the existence of institutional shareholding or do they have more institutional shareholdings because they are more profitable? It is also necessary to answer the questions: Why should managers in financial institutions be more sensitive to profit performance than the managers in the companies in which shareholdings are taken, and what does the typical institutional investor do, qua shareholder? Wide dispersion of shareholdings in institutions and an absence of residual claim- ant status on the part of their managers may create the same principal-agent problems.

A parallel line of argument occurs in the buy-out market-place.[2] The use of highly geared financial arrangements and

[1] A. Cosh, A. Hughes, M. S. Kumar and A. Singh, paper presented to ESRC Industrial Economics Study Group, University of Nottingham, Spring 1986.

[2] H. De Angelo, L. De Angelo and E. M. Rice, 'Shareholder Wealth and Going Private', *Journal of Law and Economics*, 1984, and M. C. Jensen, 'Agency Costs of Free Cash Flow, Corporate Finance and Takeovers', *American Economic Review Papers and Proceedings*, May 1986, pp. 323-29.

the conditions attached to them may require managements in buy-outs to bond themselves to a particular performance path. In buy-outs of subsidiaries from parent groups, institutional shareholdings, frequently with a non-executive director on the firm's board, may provide a 'quasi-internal' arrangement which replaces a failing internal capital market. The nature of institutional financiers may emphasise minimising downside risk rather than encouraging entrepreneurial behaviour, and may be accompanied by a requirement to dispose of 'surplus' assets. It may also be difficult to separate the influence on performance of bonding arrangements from the result of management for the first time having an equity stake in the business.

In the UK, institutional shareholders have not in general sought to intervene directly in the performance of companies in which they own shares. The recent development of management buy-outs has brought a much more active role by institutions. However, the common requirement for a withdrawal by institutions within less than three to five years may emphasise short-term goals at the expense of longer-term performance. Of course there are positive aspects to a close relationship with financing institutions, which are also interested in a return on their funds. A rapid turnover of funds, using gains from realising one project to invest in another, may be the most appropriate way for them to achieve their targets, but it is not necessarily the best approach to improve the longer-term performance of the economy in general.

Financial institutions and 'short-termism'

At the annual conference of the Confederation of British Industry (CBI) in November 1986, delegates debated a motion calling on the Government and the financial institutions to recognise that industry's performance needed to be judged over the long term rather than having a short-term view forced on managers. The conference was so divided that the Chairman decided not to count the vote. Another resolution (not discussed through lack of time) called on the conference to deplore the greed of the City and the lack of understanding displayed by those involved in providing capital to industry. As a result of these discussions the CBI launched a campaign to try to bring about a greater understanding between the City and industry.

The principal issue is the view of managers in industry that institutional investors give undue weight to the short-term performance of a company in which they place their funds. Such criticism is particularly directed at those institutions, such as pension funds and life assurance companies, which might be expected to take a rather longer view of their investments. It is argued that this short-term pressure makes managers reluctant to invest in capital projects, particularly those relating to research and development, where the returns may not be realised for some considerable time. This concern echoes a view expressed by the Wilson Committee on the functioning of financial institutions:

'... we are agreed about the importance of encouraging the long-term investment institutions to become more knowledgeable about industry and its requirements and to take a more positive attitude about their responsibilities for monitoring the performance of the companies in which they invest and for supporting and promoting their future development'.[1]

It is further argued that the fear of takeover increases the pressure on management to sacrifice long-term benefits for short-run gains. Thus, as Jensen states:

'Recent versions of the myopic markets hypothesis emphasise increasing institutional holdings and the pressures they face to generate high returns on a quarter-to-quarter basis. It is argued that these pressures on institutions are a major cause of pressures on corporations to generate high current earnings on a quarter-to-quarter basis. The institutional pressures are said to lead to increased takeovers of firms (because institutions are not loyal shareholders) and to decreased research and development expenditures. It is argued that because R&D expenditures reduce current earnings, firms making them are therefore more likely to be taken over, and that reductions in R&D are leading to a fundamental weakening of the corporate sector of the economy'.[2]

It is now appropriate, therefore, to examine these issues in more detail and consider the available evidence.

In an important study McConnell and Muscarella[3] found

[1] Committee to Review the Functioning of Financial Institutions, *Report*, Cmnd. 7937, HMSO, 1980, p. 267, para. 972.
[2] M. C. Jensen, 'The Takeover Controversy: Analysis and Evidence', in J. Coffee, L. Lowenstein and S. Rose-Ackerman (eds.), *Takeovers and Contests for Corporate Control*, Oxford University Press, 1987.
[3] J. J. McConnell and C. J. Muscarella, 'Corporate Capital Expenditure Decisions and the Market Value of the Firm', *Journal of Financial Economics*, Vol. 14, No. 3, September 1985, pp. 399-422.

that announcements of increases in planned capital expenditures are associated with statistically significant increases in the market value of ordinary shares, and announcements of reductions in planned capital expenditures with statistically significant decreases. Their evidence, therefore, contradicts the view that markets behave myopically. The findings are consistent with the large body of literature supporting the case that capital markets are efficient.[1]

US evidence favourable to institutional shareholding

In a recent study, the Office of the Chief Economist of the American Securities and Exchange Commission reported the following conclusions:[2]

— Increased institutional shareholdings are not associated with increased takeovers of firms.

— Increased institutional holdings are not associated with decreases in research and development expenditures.

— Firms with high research and development expenditures are not more vulnerable to takeovers.

— Share prices respond positively to announcements of increases in research and development expenditures.

The study related to US experience and the picture may be rather different in the UK, although American industry has been making similar points to those raised at the CBI Conference. In addition, capital markets have become more international in nature and thus any pressures are increasingly likely to be common across the main exchanges. Indeed, as a *Financial Times* leader argued, 'British industry is simply being asked to meet international standards of financial performance'.[3] The UK Stock Exchange appears to value growth as well as current earnings, as is shown by the wide variation in price/earnings ratios both within and between sectors.

Financial innovations have, if anything, increased the threat of takeovers and, as noted earlier, even large firms are susceptible to bids from smaller companies. If the market for corporate

---

[1] For example, the extensive review in E. Elton and M. Gruber, *Modern Portfolio Theory and Investment Analysis*, Wiley, New York, 1984.

[2] 'Institutional Ownership, Tender Offers and Long-Term Investments', 19 April 1985.

[3] *Financial Times*, 12 November 1986, p. 24.

control leads to improvements in the use of assets and changed business practices, it has to be recognised that 'poor' management is likely to seek refuge in arguments that the rules of the game are fair and the pressures unrealistic. As the *Financial Times* argued in commenting on the CBI Conference: 'The complaints of the loudest critics sounded a little like those of a wronged wife'.[1]

Further, it is by no means the case that short-run and long-run performance are mutually exclusive options. If resources are being used inefficiently, improvements will enhance the economic health of the firm and increase the viability of long-term projects. There is no solid evidence to date that the activities of the financial institutions or the market have led to reductions in research and development expenditure or other long-term projects which are economically viable.

In a speech in December 1986, Sir Gordon Borrie, the Director General of Fair Trading, said the fact that market forces were driven by shareholders and a myriad of financial advisers and experts

> 'does not encourage me to believe that their decisions to buy or sell particular shares at a particular price will necessarily bring about the most efficient deployment of and development of the assets which those shares represent'.

Two points should be noted about this argument: first, no institutional arrangement can ever be perfect and mistakes will always be made. The question is, therefore, what mechanisms are available for correcting such mistakes and how quickly do they operate? Secondly, what is the evidence to suggest that some other myriad body of people (such as the Office of Fair Trading or the Monopolies Commission) would make better decisions? Past experience of government decisions on industrial development would suggest that scepticism is in order.

Change and competition in financial services market

The investment activities of the institutional investors cannot be considered in isolation from developments within their own markets for the financial services and products they supply.[2] Most financial services, despite their apparent diver-

[1] *Financial Times, ibid.*
[2] For an extended discussion, M. K. Lewis, 'Financial Services in the United States', in R. L. Carter, B. Chiplin and M. K. Lewis, *op. cit.*

sity, are directed to three ends:

(i) transaction and payment services;

(ii) wealth accumulation and the ability to spread consumption over different time-periods;

(iii) financial security.

Institutions have discovered that financial services can be quite easily substituted towards these ends. Securities houses which sold products directed towards long-term savings found that the mutual fund concept could be modified and allied to payments services. Banks and other deposit-taking institutions have responded by providing new products which are better suited to medium-term savings, whilst at the same time offering some chequing facilities as shown by the introduction of high-interest cheque accounts in the UK. In a period which has been marked by variable and uncertain interest rates, short-term savings in products which bear interest rates closely related to those in wholesale money markets provide a safe and reasonably remunerative avenue for longer-term savings. Thus, new financial products have overlapped into the 'investment sector' of financial markets. Financial institutions are facing greater competition in their product markets and the introduction of more flexible investment vehicles has possibly increased the short-term pressure on fund managers. Hence, to some extent it might be argued that the investment behaviour of institutions is simply reflecting the requirements of their clients.

Developments in financial markets have probably led to an increased search for short-term results which is exacerbated by the growing internationalisation of financial markets, but it requires careful analysis to distinguish rhetoric from fact. For example, long-term loans from financial institutions, such as provided by banks in Germany, require the company to earn at least the specified rate of interest on a regular basis. As Jensen notes,[1] debt finance places managers under strong pressure to achieve results in the short term. It is by no means clear that long-term projects for which UK managers claim they are unable to obtain finance would necessarily meet the lending criteria of institutions in other countries. Capital

[1] M. C. Jensen, 'Agency Costs of Free Cash Flow, Corporate Finance and Take-overs', *American Economic Review Papers and Proceedings*, May 1986.

markets are international and many foreign financial institutions operate in the London market.

It may be that increased competition in the markets for financial products has heightened the pressure on fund managers to produce short-term performance. Likewise, they are looking for results from the companies in which they invest. Such trends are observable in several countries and are not unique to the UK. The view that UK financial markets, taken as a whole, impose unnecessarily short-term pressures on firms to the detriment of their long-run performance therefore remains to be substantiated. What is clear is that there is considerable unease amongst industry about the role of the financial institutions, which requires attention.

Debt finance and 'junk bonds'

Fairly well defined conventional views exist about what capital gearing ratios are acceptable, and they differ according to the circumstances of the loan and the nature of the business. However, the number of well-publicised takeover bids financed by fixed-interest securities has caused concern in some quarters. The fears of the potential effects of increased gearing have been most forcefully expressed in the United States where estimates suggest that the increased financing by debt of mergers and buy-outs reduced the equity base of US corporations in 1984 by some $100 billion. In the UK the bid by Elders IXL for Allied-Lyons was referred to the Monopolies Commission on the ground that the financing arrangements rested on debt capital.

In the USA so-called 'junk bonds' have attracted considerable interest. The term 'junk' is itself rather a misnomer, since it implies that these bonds are worthless, which, in practice, is far from the case. Such bonds may be defined as high-interest debt which is generally secured not against assets but against the shares in the company being acquired. In the UK, the rapidly growing management buy-out market-place has seen an element of this kind of financing through the introduction of a 'mezzanine' or layer of finance between shareholders' funds and secured debt. The provider of such high-interest unsecured loan funding may require an equity stake as an incentive. Since a company financed by high gearing will be required to meet substantial debt-servicing costs it is common for such arrangements to take place where firms have large positive and stable cash flows.

In the market for corporate control funding through high gearing can have two particularly important advantages. First, a relatively small company obtaining substantial debt finance may be enabled to acquire a much larger firm. As such, the existence of highly leveraged bids (i.e., a high proportion of debt) may reduce the protection against takeover afforded by size,[1] and such a threat may encourage more efficient management. Secondly, management of a firm with high gearing may be effectively 'bonded' to operate efficiently in order to meet debt repayment schedules, with a threat of removal if they fail. Thus, debt finance helps to reduce the agency costs associated with the divorce between ownership and control.[2]

The £1·8 billion bid by Elders IXL for Allied Lyons in 1986 provides an example of a company funding an acquisition with substantial amounts of borrowed funds. In clearing the merger the Monopolies Commission considered that the projected capital gearing ratios of between 114 and 191 per cent were not unacceptable, despite the unease expressed by the Bank of England in its evidence. The reasons for taking this view concerned the nature of the acquisition, which was of a mature company with a stable cash flow; the intention to sell-off a substantial division, so quickly reducing the capital gearing; the commercial strength and significance of Elders; and its past record in handling such situations. Moreover, the willingness of the institutions to lend on such a proposition indicated that they considered the merged group to be financially viable.

The Monopolies Commission also commented on the wider implications of this kind of financing arrangement. Whilst recognising that other highly geared bids could occur in less favourable circumstances, the Commission did not consider there was an adequate basis to suggest important changes in commercial practice, or in the law. But the Commission felt that the Bank of England, the Stock Exchange and the Department of Trade and Industry should examine the possibilities

---

[1] As discussed in Section VII, there is some evidence that in the past increased size has offered more protection against takeover than increased profit.

[2] M. C. Jensen, 'Agency Costs . . .', *op. cit.*

and need for enhanced control were highly geared bids to become a feature of the UK corporate finance scene. There are difficulties in using capital gearing ratios as a guide for control purposes, since the complex array of financing types used to fund such purchases gives substantial room for manoeuvre in calculating gearing.

Debt financing and UK takeovers

Table 9 illustrates the pattern of the financing of takeovers since 1969. The major source of payment is cash; the proportion of expenditure financed by fixed interest securities is

TABLE 9

FUNDING OF MERGERS, 1969 TO 1985,
AND 1986 (to 3rd Quarter)

	Expenditure £million				% of total expenditure		
	Total	Cash	Issues of ordinary shares	Issues of fixed interest securities	Cash	Issues of ordinary shares	Issues of fixed interest securities
1969	1,069	296	552	221	27·7	51·6	20·7
1970	1,222	251	596	275	22·4	53·1	24·5
1971	911	285	437	189	31·3	48·0	20·7
1972	2,532	493	1,459	580	19·5	57·6	22·9
1973	1,304	691	466	147	53·0	35·7	11·3
1974	508	347	114	47	68·3	22·4	9·3
1975	291	173	93	25	59·4	32·0	8·6
1976	448	321	120	7	71·7	26·8	1·5
1977	824	512	304	8	62·1	36·9	1·0
1978	1,140	654	463	23	57·4	40·6	2·0
1979	1,656	933	515	208	56·3	31·1	12·6
1980	1,475	760	669	46	51·5	45·4	3·1
1981	1,144	775	338	31	67·7	29·6	2·7
1982	2,206	1,283	701	222	58·1	31·8	10·1
1983	2,343	1,026	1,261	56	43·8	53·8	2·4
1984	5,474	2,946	1,838	690	53·8	33·6	12·6
1985	7,090	2,857	3,708	525	40·3	52·3	7·4
1986/Q3	11,302	1,702	7,252	2,348	15·1	64·2	20·8

Source: Business Monitor MQ7.

relatively low and has fallen considerably since the early 1970s. For the five years from 1969 to 1973 on average some 20 per cent of acquisition expenditure was financed by fixed interest securities; from 1981 to 1985 the proportion fell to 7 per cent. The financing of takeovers through fixed interest debt has not, therefore, been particularly important in the UK.

Those sceptical about the use of high gearing and, in particular, the use of 'junk bonds' point to the risk of default. Where companies find it difficult to meet debt repayment schedules arising, for example, from over-optimistic projections of cash-flow, given uncertain market conditions, some revision of the financial package may be possible. This restructuring may also be used where new and unanticipated investment opportunities arise. In making the loans, financial institutions will have weighed the risk-return trade-off and found it acceptable. If the general commercial judgement of such institutions is in question, then alternative control mechanisms have to be sought.

Early in 1986 the US Federal Reserve Board introduced a 'margin rule' limiting to 50 per cent the proportion of any loan for buying shares that can be secured against the shares in the company being acquired. Such a move was designed to prevent 'irresponsible' opportunistic takeovers of companies using 'other people's money'. William Proxmire, who became Chairman of the Senate Banking Committee in Autumn 1986, has also given support to such a rule.[1] Such an approach appears to be an over-reaction and the dangers of failure or heavy debt burdens must be weighed against the potential losses if corporate managements are protected artificially from the spur to efficiency that derives from the threat of takeover and the 'bonding' of performance deriving from debt capital.

[1] Interview in *The Times*, 2 December 1986.

VII. THE EFFECTS OF MERGERS

In this section some aspects of the economic effects of mergers are considered, particularly their impact on markets and on performance, both financial and real.

Concentration

The term 'concentration' relates to two different concepts:

(i) *aggregate concentration* — which is concerned with the importance of large firms in the economy and is measured by, for example, the share of net assets owned by the 100 largest firms;

(ii) *market concentration*—which relates to the relative shares of firms producing goods or services for a particular market and is measured by, for example, the proportion of output in a market produced by, say, the five largest firms.

The 20th century has witnessed a significant rise in both market and aggregate concentration in the UK and there is no doubt that mergers have made a substantial contribution to the growth of firms over the whole period.[1] As noted earlier, firms can grow by means of internal expansion as well as through acquisition. The net contribution of the two to changes in concentration has been a matter of considerable debate. Much of the initial evidence on this question came from the United States where the early merger movements were much more widespread. This American evidence, although a matter of some controversy,[2] suggests that, whilst the merger wave at the end of the 19th century fundamentally altered the structure of particular industries, the general picture is that mergers had little effect on the degree of concentration. Simi-

---

[1] For example, Leslie Hannah, *The Rise of the Corporate Economy*, Methuen, London, 2nd Edition, 1983, and M. S. Kumar, *Growth, Acquisition and Investment: An Analysis of the Growth of Industrial Firms and Their Overseas Activities*, Cambridge University Press, Cambridge, 1984.

[2] R. L. Nelson, *Merger Movements in American Industry*, Princeton University Press, Princeton, N.J., 1959; J. F. Weston, *The Role of Mergers in the Growth of Large Firms*, University of California Press, California, 1952; and G. J. Stigler, 'The Statistics on Monopoly and Mergers', *Journal of Political Economy*, 1956.

larly, in the UK the evidence suggests that, whilst mergers had a profound effect on some trades in the first part of this century, the total impact was relatively minor.[1] Thus, Hart and Prais confirmed that the pattern in the UK between 1896 and 1950 amongst quoted companies was similar to that in the USA, and suggested that changes in business concentration over time were affected more by internal than by external growth of companies. Given this evidence that mergers did not seem to have a substantial impact on concentration, it is perhaps not altogether surprising that in many countries (including the UK) merger policy was a rather late addition to the anti-trust armoury.

Since the Second World War research has shown mergers making a far more substantial contribution to changes in concentration. Thus, in examining the period from 1958 to 1968, Hart and Clarke[2] conclude that roughly half the increase in concentration was the result of merger activity. The 1978 Green Paper[3] confirmed that since the late 1950s mergers have contributed at least one-half of the increase in concentration. One important study[4] estimated that mergers accounted for more than 100 per cent of the increase between 1957 and 1967 so that concentration would have fallen in the absence of mergers. There are, however, good reasons to believe that this figure is over-stated.[5]

Argument about the precise contribution of mergers should not cloud the finding that there is now overwhelming evidence that mergers have had the effect of increasing the level of both market and aggregate concentration above what it would otherwise have been. In the late 1970s and early 1980s there seems to have been some stability in the degree of aggregate concentration in the UK,[6] but, as has been seen, merger

[1] P. E. Hart and S. J. Prais, 'The Analysis of Business Concentration: a Statistical Approach', *Journal of the Royal Statistical Society*, Series A, 1956.

[2] P. E. Hart and R. Clarke, *Concentration in British Industry, 1935–1975*, Cambridge University Press, Cambridge, 1980.

[3] *A Review of Monopolies and Mergers Policy: A Consultative Document*, Cmnd. 7198, HMSO, May 1978.

[4] L. Hannah and J. A. Kay, *Concentration in Modern Industry*, Macmillan, London, 1977.

[5] P. E. Hart, 'On Bias and Concentration', *Journal of Industrial Economics*, 1979.

[6] A. Hughes and M. S. Kumar, 'Recent Trends in Aggregate Concentration in the United Kingdom Economy', and 'Recent Trends in Aggregate Concentration in the UK Economy: Revised Estimates', *Cambridge Journal of Economics*, September and December 1984.

[63]

activity was low during this period. In recent years the volume of diversifying activity has increased, but this has less of an impact on market concentration and there appears to be no systematic relationship between mergers and diversification.[1] These results relate to periods before the start of the latest wave of mergers in 1984. To what extent mergers have again increased concentration remains to be seen, but the size of acquisitions since 1984 would lead one to expect a significant rise at least in aggregate concentration. Rising concentration of both types causes concern because of the impact on market power, the possible misallocation of resources and general concern with the potential effects of concentrated economic power in the hands of a few firms. The case-by-case approach to merger policy is not suited to deal with a series of mergers which, taken one-by-one may have little impact, but in total significantly increase aggregate concentration. The Monopolies Commission itself has expressed concern on this issue in its reports on newspaper mergers where, despite unease about the general increase in concentration, it was unable to find any particular case to be against the public interest.[2]

Characteristics of firms

A number of studies in the UK have sought to examine the characteristics of acquired and acquiring firms to discover any significant differences between three groups (i.e., acquiring, acquired and non-acquired) and to throw light on the motives for merger.[3] Although the studies refer to different time-periods

[1] Alan Hughes, 'The Impact of Merger: A Survey for the UK', paper presented at Institute of Fiscal Studies conference on Acquisitions and Mergers, London, 16 July 1986.

[2] For example, *Berrow's Organisation and County Express*, 1972, paras. 75 and 76.

[3] The studies are: H. B. Rose and G. D. Newbould, 'The 1967 Takeover Boom', *Moorgate and Wall Street*, 1967, pp. 5-24; G. D. Newbould, *Management and Merger Activity*, Guthstead Press, Liverpool, 1970; Ajit Singh, *Takeovers*, Cambridge University Press, London, 1971; A. Buckley, 'A Profile of Industrial Acquisitions in 1971', *Accounting and Business Research*, Autumn 1972, pp. 243-52; J. Tzaonnos and J. M. Samuels, 'Mergers and Takeovers: The Financial Characteristics of Companies Involved', *Journal of Business Finance*, Autumn 1972, pp. 5-16; M. A. Utton, 'On Measuring the Effects of Industrial Mergers', *Scottish Journal of Political Economy*, February 1974, pp. 13-28; Ajit Singh, 'Takeovers, Economic Natural Selection and the Theory of the Firm: Evidence from the Postwar United Kingdom Experience', *Economic Journal*, September 1975, pp. 497-515; D. A. Kuehn, *Takeovers and the Theory of the Firm*, Macmillan, London, 1975; G. Meeks, *Disappointing Marriage: A Study of Gains from Merger*, Cambridge University Press, London, 1977; P. Levine and S. Aaronovitch, 'The Financial Characteristics of Firms and Theories of Merger Activity', *Journal of Industrial Economics*, December 1981, pp. 149-73.

and use varying methodologies, a number of conclusions are possible. Most studies find that the profitability of acquired firms is lower than the average, but there are two exceptions: Meeks in his study, which covered 1964-71, found that the typical victim was about average in terms of profitability, as did Levine and Aaronovitch for mergers in 1972. A majority find that the valuation ratio of acquired firms also tends to be low. The general conclusion, however, is that there is a considerable overlap in the financial characteristics between the three groups and it is not easy to distinguish between them. In general the best indicator appears to be size—smaller firms are more likely to be taken over—and hence the best way to avoid a takeover is to grow bigger.

However, one needs to be careful in interpreting this type of research. In the market for corporate control the *threat* of takeover is supposed to stir management to greater efforts to improve efficiency and to maximise value for shareholders. If the market worked perfectly, therefore, there would be no takeovers for this reason, since the threat alone would be sufficient. Mergers which take place would be for other reasons so that we would not expect to observe any systematic relationship between financial variables and the probability of takeover.

The characteristics of the acquiring group are also rather indistinct, although there is some evidence to suggest they are generally more dynamic (higher growth rates) and of average or above average profitability.

All these studies refer to a much earlier period and there is no evidence covering the mid-1980s. The same conclusion applies to the studies of post-merger performance which are examined next.

Post-merger performance

Measures of post-merger performance can be considered under three headings:

(i) accounting rates of return;
(ii) real cost per unit of output; and
(iii) change in share prices.

(i) Accounting rates of return

Several studies in the UK have sought to assess the impact of merger on the profitability of the combined company. Post-merger profitability can increase for one of two reasons: a reduction in real costs or a rise in prices relative to costs. Since the latter can result from an increase in market power consequent upon the merger, a rise in profitability does not prove that efficiency has necessarily increased. On the other hand, if profitability declines it is possible to conclude that efficiency has fallen.[1]

Singh[2] compared the combined pre-merger profitability with the post-merger rate of return adjusted for the industry average. He found that for a sample of 77 firms during the period 1955-60 two-thirds had lower profits in the year of the merger than previously. In the first, second and third years after merger a substantial number also experienced reduced profitability. He concluded that in at least a half of the cases there was a decline in profitability after the merger. To allow for multiple acquirers, Utton[3] took a sample of 39 firms which had been intensive acquirers during 1961-65 and which then subsequently expanded to the end of the decade primarily through internal growth. He concluded that companies heavily dependent on acquisitions had a lower rate of return in subsequent periods. Utton did not adjust his results to reflect the underlying profitability of the industry of the company, and neither study made an adjustment for 'goodwill' which resulted from the premium over book value of the acquired firm's assets. Consequently, post-merger assets were generally artificially over-valued, thereby reducing the rate of return.

A comprehensive study by Meeks[4] for the period 1964-72 sought to deal with these problems. His sample covered 233 larger quoted companies and, after allowing for industry profits and goodwill, he found that between one-half and two-thirds of companies in the sample experienced a decline in profits each year after the merger. Once a firm acquired a second company it was dropped from the sample and hence Meeks's results apply to single-firm mergers only. As such there is an element of self-selection in the sample in that companies which have found acquisition a profitable activity are likely to engage in further ventures. However, the general

[1] G. Meeks and J. G. Meeks, 'Profitability Measures as Indicators of Post-Merger Efficiency', *Journal of Industrial Economics*, June 1981, pp. 335-44.

[2] Ajit Singh, *Takeovers, op. cit.*

[3] M. A. Utton, 'On Measuring the Effects of Industrial Mergers', *op. cit.*

[4] G. Meeks, *Disappointing Marriage, op. cit.*

tenor of the findings is unlikely to be changed on this account. Kumar[1] reaches similar conclusions based on a sample of 354 mergers, although he does take care to introduce the necessary qualifications:

'Since, in general, profitability declined after merger, even under the assumption of unchanged monopoly power, this may be taken to suggest no efficiency gains, and indeed some deterioration. It is very important to emphasise, however, that the evidence is much more ambiguous than this. First, in a significant minority of cases profitability actually improved after merger. Second, even where there was a decline, the magnitude of the decline was in general small. In any case the changes in profitability have to be seen in relation to other dynamic effects, such as the effect on investment or exports. The strongest guide to monopoly policy would be given if, for example, both profitability and investment performance worsened in the vast majority of cases, and worsened considerably. The evidence does not suggest this to have been the case'.[2]

Littlechild[3] also offers a number of qualifications to the profitability studies. In particular he emphasises that they generally assume that pre-merger profit rates would have been maintained, and yet many mergers take place precisely because the firms concerned do not expect this to be possible. Moreover, if mergers result in a rationalising of the structure of an industry, they may lead to a rise in profitability across all firms in that sector. Hence, the 'unprofitability' of mergers may have been over-estimated.

The accounting findings are consistent with work which has used a questionnaire approach.[4] These studies have shown that a majority of the managers concerned regard the mergers as unsuccessful.

Apart from the problem of interpretation alluded to earlier, many difficulties are involved in using accounting data to measure company performance after merger. Meeks and Meeks[5] identify a number of sources of bias including changes

[1] M. S. Kumar, *Growth, Acquisition and Investment*, *op. cit.*

[2] *Ibid.*, pp. 181-2.

[3] S. C. Littlechild, 'Some Suggestions for UK Competition Policy', in *Agenda for Social Democracy*, Hobart Paperback No. 15, Institute of Economic Affairs, 1983, pp. 89-110.

[4] For example, G. Newbould, *Management and Merger Activity*, *op. cit.*, and J. Kitching, 'Why Acquisitions are Abortive', *Management Today*, November 1974.

[5] G. Meeks and J. G. Meeks, 'Profitability Measures as Indicators of Post-Merger Efficiency', *op. cit.*

in bargaining power, inter-company sales, and changes in gearing which are likely seriously to distort any accounting measures of the effects of mergers. It is for this reason, amongst others, that much recent work has concentrated on the effect of mergers on share prices, and how share price data can be used to test various hypotheses about the impact of mergers.

(ii) *Real cost effects*

One alternative to the use of accounting profitability data[1] is to seek to analyse whether real costs per unit fall as a result of merger. The case study work of Cowling and his colleagues at Warwick University established the basic methodology and reported the results of a number of investigations into horizontal mergers.[2] As it is detailed case study material it is difficult to do justice to the results in a brief summary, but the general impression is that gains in efficiency as a direct result of merger do not seem to have been forthcoming in a majority of cases. In addition, there was little evidence that economies of scale contributed to gains in efficiency. Thus:

'. . . it is difficult to sustain the view that merger is in fact a necessary or sufficient condition for efficiency gain. In many cases efficiency has not improved, in some cases it has declined, in other cases it has improved but no faster than one would have expected in the absence of merger . . . There are one or two cases where we have seen an efficiency gain which has followed from the merger, these cases being where superior management has gained control over more resources'.[3]

(iii) *Stock market studies*

A vast number of studies, particularly in the United States, have investigated the effects of mergers on the stock market value of shares.[4] A common approach is to use an events-

---

[1] Although it is subject to some of the same biases as shown by G. Meeks and J. G. Meeks, *ibid.*

[2] K. Cowling *et al.*, *Mergers and Economic Performance*, Cambridge University Press, Cambridge, 1980, and J. Cubbin and G. Hall, 'The Use of Real Cost as an Efficiency Measure: An Application to Merging Firms', *Journal of Industrial Economics*, September 1979, pp. 73-88.

[3] K. Cowling *et al.*, *ibid.*, p. 370.

[4] For a comprehensive survey of those undertaken up to 1983, M. C. Jensen and R. S. Ruback, 'The Market for Corporate Control: The Scientific Evidence', *Journal of Financial Economics*, April 1983, pp. 5-50.

based methodology[1] whereby the share price around some event (such as a merger) is examined for the presence of abnormal returns in relation to what might have been expected from the trends in the market. The market model posits a linear relationship between the return (capital gains plus dividends) on an individual security and the return available in the market as measured by a market index.[2] The predicted return can be derived in a number of alternative ways, including an adjustment for risk.[3] Such analyses are based on the efficient markets hypothesis, namely that a share price fully incorporates all available information on the security and that share prices therefore provide accurate signals for optimal allocation of resources.[4] Thus, share prices will correctly reflect the economic value of the share, given the available information.

Compared to the American literature, the number of studies of UK share prices in response to takeovers is rather limited.[5]

---

[1] For an overview, S. J. Brown and J. B. Warner, 'Using Daily Stock Returns: The Case of Event Studies', *Journal of Financial Economics*, 1985, pp. 3-31.

[2] This relationship can be expressed as follows:

$$R_{it} = a_i + B_i R_{mt} + u_{it}$$

where R_{it} is the rate of return on firm i in period t and R_{mt} is the rate of return on a market index. The coefficients (a and B) are usually estimated by ordinary least squares regression for a set of data where a period around the event date has been deleted. The difference between the predicted returns estimated by this market model and the actual returns are compared to obtain an estimate of abnormal returns around the merger. Thus

$$u_{it} = R_{it} - [a_i + B_i R_{mt}].$$

[3] For example, Paul Halpern, 'Corporate Acquisitions: A Theory of Special Cases? A Review of Event Studies Applied to Acquisitions', *Journal of Finance*, May 1983, pp. 297-317.

[4] E. F. Fama, 'Efficient Capital Markets: A Review of Theory and Empirical Work', *Journal of Finance*, May 1970.

[5] The most notable are: J. R. Franks, J. E. Broyles and M. J. Hecht, 'An Industry Study of the Profitability of Mergers in the UK', *Journal of Finance*, December 1977, pp. 1,513-1,525; P. Barnes, 'The Effect of Merger on the Share Price of the Attacker', *Accounting and Business Research*, Summer 1978, pp. 162-65; M. Firth, 'The Profitability of Takeovers and Mergers', *Economic Journal*, June 1979, pp. 316-28; M. Firth, 'Takeovers, Shareholder Returns and the Theory of the Firm', *Quarterly Journal of Economics*, March 1980, pp. 235-60; P. Barnes, 'The Effect of Merger on the Share Price of the Attacker Re-visited', *Accounting and Business Research*, Winter 1984, pp. 45-49; J. C. Dodds and J. P. Quek, 'Effect of Mergers on the Share Price Movement of the Acquiring Firms: A UK Study', *Journal of Business Finance and Accounting*, Summer 1985, pp. 285-96; and J. R. Franks and R. S. Harris, 'Shareholder Wealth Effects of Corporate Takeovers: The UK Experience 1955-85', paper presented to Institute of Fiscal Studies conference on Mergers and Acquisitions, London, 16 July 1986.

The study by Franks, Broyles and Hecht was based on a single industry—brewing and distilling for the period 1955-72. They found considerable evidence that the shareholders in the target firm gained from the merger and there was no evidence that shareholders in the acquiring firm suffered any loss. They argued that the gains on combined shareholding in both acquirer and target company reflected net gains from merging within the industry. They also found that the market began to anticipate mergers at least three months, on average, before they were announced. A study by Firth[1] examined the period 1972-74 and found little or no total gain or loss associated with takeovers; the large positive gains to shareholders in the target company were almost exactly counterbalanced by losses to the owners of the acquirer. He concluded that the market appears to think that takeovers will not lead to any private economic gains:

> '... the stock market is expecting little change in the profitability of firms once they have combined; any possible benefits in the form of synergy or reorganisation of the acquired firm are presumably being countered by doubts of whether the offeror has access to management capable of greatly increasing efficiency, and because of the costs involved in the takeover process'.

Gains for shareholders in acquired firms

Dodds and Quek used a sample of 70 companies for the period 1974-76 and concluded that acquiring firms experienced an increase in their share price relative to the market for the first 25 months following the announcement, but thereafter the price fell sharply, indicating a change in expectations as new information became available. The most recent and comprehensive study is that of Franks and Harris which covers a sample of 1,898 firms acquired over the period January 1955 to June 1985. Their results show sizeable premiums on acquisition and support the contention that shareholders in acquired companies gain substantially in mergers. Mergers are neutral or slightly beneficial to the shareholders in the acquiring firm and hence there are net gains to equity owners. The bid premiums for the acquiree's shareholders are higher in revised or contested bids, and when the acquiring company holds a pre-merger equity interest in the target. On post-merger performance, they conclude:

[1] 'Takeovers, Shareholder Returns and the Theory of the Firm', *op. cit.*

[70]

'Evidence suggests that over the two years subsequent to merger, acquirers have returns comparable to general stock market results. These returns do not, however, keep pace with the acquirer's own pre-merger performance. Though in need of future research, these results suggest that acquirers may time takeovers to coincide with favourable performance of their stock'.[1]

Thus, with the exception of Firth the studies in the UK suggest that the stock market expects positive economic gains from the merger although, given the longer-term evidence of Dodds and Quek, there must be some doubt whether these expectations are realised; a point which is re-inforced by consideration of profitability and real costs.

How does British experience compare with that in other countries, particularly the USA? In their major survey of the empirical evidence Jensen and Ruback conclude:

'In brief, the evidence seems to indicate that corporate takeovers generate positive gains, that target firm shareholders benefit, and that bidding firm shareholders do not lose. Moreover, the gains created by corporate takeovers do not appear to come from the creation of market power'.[2]

In a recent study, Dennis and McConnell[3] extend the analysis to include other classes of security holder in America. From a sample of 132 mergers between 1962 and 1980 they conclude that several classes of security holders in acquired companies gain as a result, namely common stockholders, convertible and non-convertible preferred stockholders, and convertible bondholders. Most classes of security holders in acquiring firms neither gain nor lose. The ordinary shareholders in acquiring companies appear to gain. Their evidence, therefore, supports the view that mergers are on average value-creating, which they argue is consistent with the existence of synergy.

In an interesting paper, Holderness and Sheehan[4] consider

[1] J. R. Franks and R. S. Harris, 'Shareholder Wealth Effects of Corporate Takeovers: The UK Experience 1955–85', *op. cit.*

[2] M. C. Jensen and R. S. Ruback, 'The Market for Corporate Control: The Scientific Evidence', *op. cit.*, p. 47.

[3] D. K. Dennis and J. J. McConnell, 'Corporate Mergers and Security Returns', *Journal of Financial Economics*, 1986, pp. 143-87.

[4] C. G. Holderness and D. P. Sheehan, 'Raiders or Saviours? The Evidence on Six Controversial Investors', *Journal of Financial Economics*, 1985, pp. 555-79.

the activities of six controversial 'raiders' in the period 1977-82.[1] They investigate three possible hypotheses concerning their role.

The role of 'raiders'

(1) *Raiding hypothesis:* whereby the six investors purchase shares and 'raid' target firms to the detriment of other shareholders by transferring assets to themselves;

(2) *Improved management hypothesis:* whereby the six help improve the management of the target firm;

(3) *Superior security analyst hypothesis:* whereby the six, either through access to non-public information or better skills at evaluating known information, are able to identify and purchase under-priced shares.

Holderness and Sheehan, on the basis of their evidence, reject the raiding hypothesis. They conclude that announcements of initial purchases by the six were associated with increases in the wealth of target firm shareholders. As they argue:

> 'While the empirical evidence is inconsistent with the raiding hypothesis, the precise market role of the six is less clear. One reasonable interpretation of the evidence is that the six investors are associated with management changes that increase the value of corporate assets'.

In a recently published study for Canada, Eckbo[2] examines 1,900 mergers between 1964 and 1983 and concludes, in contrast to the general evidence in America, that both target and bidder firm shareholders earn significant gains from takeover activity and that these do not differ between horizontal and other types of merger.

The general picture from these studies is, therefore, that abnormal gains in share prices around the merger date indicate that the stock market expects there will be positive economic gains from takeovers. It is inappropriate in the present context to discuss in detail the limitations and drawbacks of this type of study. It is immediately apparent that determining the merger 'event' is no easy matter, particularly in the light of

[1] The six are Carl Icahn, Irwin Jacobs, Carl Lindner, David Murdoch, Victor Posner and Charles Bluhdorn.

[2] B. E. Eckbo, 'Mergers and the Market for Corporate Control: The Canadian Evidence', *Canadian Journal of Economics*, 1986, pp. 236-60.

insider trading, as discussed earlier. The choice of the under-lying model to predict share prices from which the abnormal returns are derived is also the subject of some contention.[1] In addition, there is a small firm effect in the sense that if the acquiring firm is large relative to the target then any gains or losses from the merger will tend to be swamped by the firm's other activities and a small acquisition will have little effect on the share price of the acquirer.[2] Of course, as noted earlier, the presumption that a net increase in the value of shares relative to the market indicates real economic gain is conditional on the hypothesis that the capital market is efficient.

Mergers and internal organisation of the firm

The existence of the firm in replacing market transactions with administrative decision-taking has long been seen to rest on the presence of transaction and control costs.[3] Efficiency may be improved by conducting activities within the firm rather than through a market transaction. The rationale behind this view has been examined in relation to all aspects of integration—that is, horizontal, vertical and lateral (conglomerate).

With vertical and horizontal integration, it may be argued that transactions should be internalised when a lack of trust exists, especially under conditions of complexity in the trans-action.[4] Economies from the production of multiple products (economies of scope) are more likely to arise where the specialist application of proprietary know-how is required and where physical assets are indivisible.[5] Some merger activity, therefore, may be regarded as a search procedure aimed at achieving these benefits of internalisation.

Such analyses also suggest that both labour and capital

[1] For example, Paul Halpern, *op. cit.*; S. J. Brown and J. B. Warner, *op. cit.*; and J. R. Franks and R. S. Harris, *op. cit.*

[2] For a discussion, Franks and Harris, *ibid.*

[3] For example, R. H. Coase, 'The Nature of the Firm', *Economica*, 1937, and O. E. Williamson, 'The Vertical Integration of Production: Market Failure Consider-ations', *American Economic Review Papers and Proceedings*, May 1971, and *Markets and Hierarchies*, The Free Press, New York, 1975.

[4] R. Butler and M. Carney, 'Managing Markets: The Implications for the Make-Buy Decision', *Journal of Management Studies*, 1983.

[5] D. Teece, 'Economies of Scope and the Scope of the Enterprise', *Journal of Economic Behaviour and Organization*, 1980, pp. 223-47.

productivity may be enhanced by effective administrative direction in conglomerates. Internal capital markets may be more efficient than external ones: the internal allocation of resources does not depend on the disclosure of confidential information to outsiders, and internal funding can be followed by detailed monitoring accompanied by sanctions or assistance where necessary. The external capital market, in contrast, is said to require sensitive information to assess its lending risk. To realise the benefits of internal capital allocation requires the separation of strategic investment and operating responsibilities within the firm. A suitable organisational form allows for appropriation of the benefits of the decentralised use of information, together with an incentive to reduce any cost-inflating goals of management (opportunism, shirking, etc.).

Changes in structure

These arguments have tended to stress the advantages of mergers in restructuring the firm and in generating improvements in organisational efficiency. Jensen has further argued that a new management team after a takeover may be able to introduce policies that the encumbent management would have found difficult.[1] However, there are a number of limits to what can be achieved by organisation which tend to be under-estimated in these analyses, and such arguments ignore the inherited characteristics of established organisations. As Arrow[2] has noted, established organisations are governed by a specific set of codes which may prove difficult to change— even with the introduction of new personalities. Such problems may be exacerbated when it is recognised that the informal distribution of power within a structure may not correspond to the formal organisation chart. An organisation may be dominated by a ruling coalition whose activities interfere with the rational allocation of resources. These problems have been noted particularly in the assimilation of new acquisitions into a group structure where the corporate 'culture' of the new parent is incompatible with that in the acquired firm. By contrast, in management buy-outs on divestment evidence

[1] M. C. Jensen, 'The Takeover Controversy: Analysis and Evidence', in J. Coffee, L. Lowenstein and S. Rose-Ackerman (eds.), *Takeovers and Contests for Corporate Control*, Oxford University Press, 1987 (forthcoming).

[2] K. Arrow, *The Limits to Organization*, Norton, New York, 1974.

suggests that freedom from parental control enables changes to be made which could not otherwise have happened.[1]

The control problems involved in managing trading relationships internally may also be under-estimated. A merger effected to internalise transactions and obtain the benefits of vertical or horizontal integration may fail to recognise adequately the different levels of dependence of the combined parts on each other. Problems arise where an approach to managing one part is not appropriate for others. Replacing market transactions by a hierarchy embracing constituent units of a divisionalised firm may also affect the behaviour of the trading business. Common ownership may present a barrier to entry against outside suppliers and allow an upstream process unit, for example, to 'exploit' a downstream business dependent on the upstream output. The greater the dependence of one element on the other, the bigger is the problem. Attempts may be made to strengthen internal control and co-ordination, but such a policy has its limits.

In addition to these problems of co-ordination, there is also the difficulty of effectively monitoring the behaviour of employees in an organisation because of incompletely specified labour contracts. The hirer of labour has to be able to monitor the quality and quantity of work produced in return for remuneration. The incompleteness of employee contracts may lead to dissipation of the hoped-for benefits of an internal labour market. These benefits relate, for example, to better selection achieved through internal promotion and the improved commitment obtained from employees by the possibility of such promotion. However, such benefits may not be captured since the incompleteness of contracts may enable one or other party to exploit specific circumstances to their own advantage.

Hence, mergers may not necessarily achieve the benefits of reduced costs of carrying out transactions and of control that internalisation is supposed to bring. One way around the problem may be to attempt to allow employees to participate directly in the profits earned by the organisation so as to give the incentive to perform effectively. However, although there have recently been moves to extend the use of such schemes in

---

[1] C. S. Jones, 'An Empirical Study of the Role of Management Accounting Systems Following Takeover or Merger', *Accounting, Organization and Society*, 1985, pp. 177-200, for the problem of assimilation, and M. Wright and J. Coyne, *Management Buy-outs*, Croom-Helm, Beckenham, Kent, 1985, for the evidence on buy-outs.

the UK, a review of the literature by Bradley and Gelb[1] took the view that the effect on performance is inconclusive. A major problem is to design schemes so that the rewards an employee is able to obtain are directly related to his/her *own* performance, rather than enabling the individual to free-ride on the performance of others.

Redrawing the boundaries via divestment

An alternative approach is to redraw the boundaries of the organisation so as to remove unwanted or uncontrollable parts. If mergers are seen, in part, as a search procedure, then it has to be recognised that mistakes are likely to be made. Redrawing the boundaries through divestment allows mistakes to be corrected and adjustments to be made in the light of developing circumstances. Divestment may be done in several ways: parts which are peripheral to the main activities may simply be sold to a new parent or to the subsidiary's management. Where trading relationships exist, divestment or contracting-out is possible. If this action is carried out so that the divested part is sold to a specialist in a particular activity, economies of scale may be obtained to outweigh any resulting costs of externalisation. Alternatively, divestment to management may take place through a management buy-out. Under such circumstances, competition between suppliers may become more effective as the barrier to entry of common ownership is removed. Moreover, as management now have an ownership stake in the business for which they work, an important stimulus to performance previously absent may be introduced.[2]

Where a firm perceives benefits from joint production of products but does not have the expertise, either technical, managerial or organisational, to produce the whole range, joint ventures with other firms may be preferable to merger. This consideration may particularly apply to financial services where an important aspect of increasing competition and de-regulation is the diversification of institutions away from their traditional expertise into new activities which are themselves highly competitive. Where several joint venture arrangements exist effective competition in a market may still be maintained.

[1] K. Bradley and A. Gelb, *Share Ownership for Employees*, Public Policy Centre, London, 1986.

[2] M. Wright, 'The Make-Buy Decision and Managing Markets: The Case of Management Buyouts', *Journal of Management Studies*, July 1986.

VIII. POLICY ISSUES

This discussion raises a number of important issues for the future direction of merger policy in the UK that are now developed further.

The public interest presumption

Apart from the problem of defining the public interest, which is left deliberately vague and all-encompassing by section 84 of the Fair Trading Act, UK policy has been criticised for its benign stance towards mergers. The issue was raised in a previous review of merger policy in 1978 and, despite strong arguments for a change in the burden of proof, the authors of the Green Paper recommended:

'... we do not believe that the evidence about the effects of mergers justifies a complete reversal of the presumption, applied either selectively or across the board. This would be too drastic in its effects and we do not recommend it. Instead of so drastic a change, we consider that the evidence and the UK's situation call for a shift from the present policy which tends to operate in favour of mergers to an essentially neutral approach that would have due regard to the dangers of abuse of market power resulting from reduced competition and to the possible dangers of further increases in aggregate concentration, but would also recognise the economic benefits that may accrue from improved industrial structure'.[1]

This proposal was not implemented. As noted earlier, the Director General of Fair Trading now appears to consider that, at least for mergers above a certain size, the burden of proof should be less benign.

Four policy options

There are four basic approaches to merger policy:[2]

[1] *A Review of Monopolies and Mergers Policy, op. cit.*, paras 5.17 and 5.18.

[2] Alan Hughes, Dennis C. Mueller and Ajit Singh, 'Competition Policy in the 1980s: The Implications of the International Merger Wave', in Dennis C. Mueller (ed.), *The Determinants and Effects of Mergers*, Oelschlager, Gunn and Hain, Cambridge, Mass., 1980.

[77]

(i) *The pro-merger approach:* the government actively encourages merger and provides appropriate tax and other incentives as well as acting as 'marriage broker' on occasion.

(ii) *The trade-off approach:* a neutral stance is taken by the government which compares, case-by-case, the likely gains in efficiency against the possible losses from increased market power.[1]

(iii) *The competitive-structure approach:* all mergers having an adverse effect on the competitive structure are prohibited irrespective of any possible efficiency gains.

(iv) *The anti-merger approach:* the government bans all mergers involving companies above a certain size unless substantial net social benefits can be demonstrated.

UK policy has tended to fluctuate between the first two with, for example, the Industrial Reorganisation Corporation encouraging mergers in the 1960s and policy being in favour of mergers rather than neutral. The Tebbit guidelines which stress competition and move somewhat towards (iii) relate, of course, only to the reference criteria; the Monopolies Commission is still required to consider the public interest. Defending the current policy, the Director General of Fair Trading has argued:

'Competition policy in the UK has always been implemented in a pragmatic way. To some commentators pragmatism is a term of abuse indicating lack of clarity and direction. But in my view, competition policy cannot be administered by reference to rigid rules or criteria'.[2]

The four alternatives just outlined omit one important view of competition and the role of merger policy, namely, that competition is a dynamic *process* and not a matter of static equilibrium. Monopoly profits provide a strong stimulus to imitation and, in the absence of entry barriers, a monopolist will remain powerful only if a competitive advantage is maintained through innovation, investment and other dynamic changes. Mergers are a crucial part of this competitive process and there is always an inherent contradiction in merger policy: any action to restrict merger activity because of possible effects

[1] O. E. Williamson, 'Economies as an Antitrust Defence: the Welfare Trade-offs', *American Economic Review*, March 1968.

[2] *British Business*, 6 June 1986, p. 444.

[78]

on market power in product markets must make the market for corporate control less competitive. The arguments for a tougher policy towards mergers in the UK are largely based on the empirical evidence that has been reviewed in this *Hobart Paper*: the lack of measured efficiency gains, the apparent lack of discipline imposed by the takeover mechanism, and the rise in concentration, both market and aggregate, are the main cornerstones of the case. Some of the qualifications that have to be attached to this evidence have already been specified.

Perhaps the major problem is that many of the gains are likely to remain unperceived, since the threat of a takeover encourages existing management to act more efficiently. Thus, for example, the performance of Distillers had worsened considerably prior to the bids by Argyll Foods and Guinness, since it had felt relatively immune from takeover because of its size.[1]

Observed mergers take place for a variety of reasons and hence may not be particularly associated with, say, profitability. Without the threat of takeover, however, the general level of efficiency in British industry might be much lower.

Failed mergers and management performance

In a recent paper, John Kay[2] has argued that this takeover mechanism has a number of drawbacks that make it an ineffective control device. The main focus of the criticism is on its cost and inefficiency—high transactions costs coupled with the failure to punish bad management. He cites the unsuccessful bid of Dixons for Woolworth, where despite a substantial bid premium (of the order of 50 per cent) the takeover was rejected by the shareholders. Such an argument is totally misleading: this particular bid, and many contested bids, are fought on the basis of which management team is judged better able to run the company *in the future*. Bygones are bygones: if the existing management is successful in resisting the bid it must be because its future performance is expected to represent a change from past behaviour and policies. If these prospects are not realised the company will again become a potential target. Thus, failed bids do not mean that the

---

[1] Ivan Fallon, 'Guinness, the brewing storm', *Sunday Times*, 1 March 1987, p. 47.

[2] Paper presented to Institute of Fiscal Studies Conference on Acquisitions and Mergers, London, 16 July 1986.

takeover mechanism is not working—they are in a real sense a manifestation of its success.

As for expense, the costs have to be balanced against the realised gains which might be expected to accrue over a number of years. The empirical evidence does not allow any realistic assessment to be made of the benefits of the takeover mechanism because the impact on behaviour and performance from the *threat* of acquisition is unobserved. Actual mergers may occur for many other reasons and cannot be used to judge the performance of the market for corporate control. As noted earlier, the current wave of substantial takeover bids has meant that only the very largest corporations can now feel immune from the threat; one only has to read the financial press to note the impact made in some company boardrooms.

John Kay also claims that there is no industrial logic in many current bids and the mechanism is self-exhausting in that there will eventually be no one left to acquire. Such arguments also miss the main point: the takeover mechanism works by threat and hence mergers do not actually have to occur for it to work. Moreover, the population of firms is not static and new potential 'targets' emerge all the time, as the scale of activity on the Unlisted Securities Market (USM) indicates. The relevance of industrial logic is also hard to see: if performance is not harmed, where is the loss to society? Further, as has been continually argued in this *Paper*, the boundaries of the firm are regularly adjusted through divestment and sale of assets.

Kay's search for an alternative to the takeover mechanism leads him to suggest a more active role for institutional investors and more effective non-executive directors. The institutions have, it is true, traditionally taken a back-seat in the management of the companies in which they invest their customers' funds, although winning their votes is crucial in any contested bid. Since their decision will presumably be swayed by their belief in the relative efficiency of the competing management teams, the winner may feel under stronger pressure than otherwise to deliver the promises. At the same time, changes in the markets for financial services are leading to increased competition in the institutions' product markets. For these reasons one might expect the role of institutional investors to increase over the next few years. Of course, there are inherent conflicts of interest: some institutions make substantial returns from putting together takeover deals; and substantial short-run gains can be made by buying shares in a low-performing company, and, rather than improve that company's profitability, some institutions may seek to sell the shares at a premium to a takeover bidder.

Divestment

The role of the sale of parts of an enterprise is frequently misunderstood. A substantial body of evidence now points to bigness as the enemy of profitability and efficiency. In Section III we discussed the importance of acquisition and divestment as part of the dynamic strategy of the firm in adapting to changing circumstances. In this section we consider the possibility of enforced divestment as an element of competition policy. Such enforced divestment can take place either pre- or post-merger.

At present there is no provision in UK merger legislation for undertakings to be given to the OFT/MMC so that, if a merger is allowed to proceed, a subsidiary that presents problems on grounds of market power would subsequently be divested. The competition authorities have no sanctions to ensure that any such undertaking would be met, except a referral to the MMC under the six-months rule. This question was raised recently in the takeover battles for Imperial, Distillers and Woolworth. It has been suggested that the following kind of procedure might be adopted.[1]

First, it would be necessary to identify with the OFT what is likely to be the offending market consequence of an intended merger with an estimate of the post-merger market shares. Second, which businesses would be required to be divested would have to be identified and a divestment plan prepared. Third, a search for a credible buyer would have to be instigated. Fourth, the OFT would have to be satisfied that effective competition would subsequently be maintained. Fifth, it would be important to demonstrate that there would be no material distortion to competition in all the markets in which the merged firms operate. Sixth, it would be necessary to ensure that if divestment were to take place, it would not hamper the continued development of the merged concerns.

[1] For example, John Swift, 'Merger Policy: Certainty or Lottery?', paper presented at Institute of Fiscal Studies Conference on Acquisitions and Mergers, London, 16 July 1986.

The power to order divestiture after a merger has been available in the UK since the 1965 Monopolies and Mergers Act and was continued as section 73 of the 1973 Fair Trading Act. The power has not been used, even though the MMC has identified situations where it might be appropriate, particularly cases where vertical integration has been used to restrict competition through creating barriers to entry. Divestiture has recently been ordered where a firm contemplating a merger has built up a substantial shareholding in its intended victim, for example, Eurocanadian Shipholdings/Furness, Withy and Great Universal Stores/Empire Stores. This process is, however, limited by the rule that divestment has to be ordered within six months of the shareholding becoming publicly known.

A strong case can be made for enforced divestment in certain circumstances.[1] Essentially, enforced divestment may be justified on the grounds of an unsatisfactory structure *per se* or as a means of dealing with the unsatisfactory conduct of a firm.

The structural approach

The structural approach to divestment has been the subject of considerable debate. Critics have pointed to several problems in the operation of a *per se* structural approach to divestment. The first concerns the definition of a market and of concentration within that market. Second, divestment will be justified only if there are significant barriers to entry, so that super-normal profits would be maintained in the long run.[2] The definition and durability of entry barriers is as contentious an issue as that of market concentration. Third, as noted in the discussion of performance, there are difficulties in using accounting data to define economic profits. Fourth, structure itself is ambiguous; although mergers may reduce the number of firms and increase concentration, they may result in the firms being more equal in size with beneficial effects on competition. Fifth, a structural approach may focus on firms capable of being divested rather than on ones which adversely affect competition. Sixth, as the structural approach ignores conduct, it

---

[1] For an excellent analysis of the issues, D. P. O'Brien, 'Divestiture: The Case of AT & T', in J. Coyne and M. Wright (eds.), *Divestment and Strategic Change*, Philip Allan, Oxford, 1986.

[2] The market is thus not subject to hit-and-run entry which would provide a competitive outcome even if dominated by a few large firms: W. J. Baumol, 'Contestable Markets: An Uprising in the Theory of Industrial Structure', *American Economic Review*, 1982, pp. 1-15.

is difficult to predict the outcome of divestment and hence the authorities may be reluctant to order it. Seventh, a structural approach may preserve the number of competitors rather than the degree of competition. Eighth, a structural approach to divestment may mean that the benefits of economies in transaction costs in large organisations will be lost.

These criticisms of the structural approach are themselves subject to difficulties. Vertical integration creates barriers to entry, including the capture of common sources of supply and price leadership by a dominant firm, leading to horizontal concentration. It may, therefore, be better to prevent or undo such mergers rather than attempt *post hoc* regulation. Preserving the number of competitors in a market may still allow the potential for competition to be maintained even if at a particular time competition is low. Moreover, as argued earlier, economies in transaction costs may be limited where large firms experience problems of co-ordination. Divestiture may work more quickly than waiting for dominant positions created by merger to be eroded by entry of new firms, or by technological change. In addition, increased concentration is not necessarily associated with improved efficiency or profitability, as the studies reviewed earlier have shown.

Even if criticisms of the structural approach are accepted, as O'Brien has forcefully argued, there may be important reasons to enforce divestment because of the conduct of firms. Undesirable conduct may indeed be traceable to structure, and apply to all three types of merged firm, including conglomerates, which have hitherto tended to be treated more favourably than horizontal integration. Conglomerates may have a large measure of power to engage in predatory pricing across a number of markets.

Divestment difficulties

If an economic case is accepted to use enforced divestment in certain circumstances, major practical issues still arise. Much of the practical experience derives from the United States where divestment has been a feature of anti-trust policy for many years.[1] The problems are concerned with the incentives

[1] For example, K. G. Elzinga and W. Breit, *The Antitrust Penalties: A Study in Law and Economics*, Yale University Press, 1976; and M. P. Pfunder, D. Plaine and A. Whittemore, 'Compliance with Divestiture Orders Under Section 7 of the Clayton Act: An Analysis of the Relief Obtained', *Antitrust Bulletin*, 1972, pp. 19-180.

for the offending firm to co-operate in divestment, the choice of assets to be divested, the incentives for anti-trust officials to carry out policy, the difficulties in finding an appropriate buyer at an acceptable price, and the penalty to shareholders.

US practice often places the burden on the offending firm to implement a divestment order. There is a clear incentive for such firms to delay the process by asking an excessive price for the divested part. Experience has also shown that it is necessary to divest an economically viable set of assets, which may be difficult to disentangle from an integrated entity. The careers of anti-trust officials are more likely to be advanced by winning cases rather than by effective implementation of divestment rulings. Apart from finding a buyer willing to accept the price demanded by the divestor, it is important that the acquiror does not also infringe anti-trust legislation. Whether or not shareholders should effectively be penalised for the actions of management is a contentious issue in the divestment literature. US experience has tended to leave it to the courts to avoid penalising shareholders. Empirical studies[1] suggest that shareholders do not necessarily lose and may indeed be better off. Increasingly, the parts of a firm may be worth more than the whole. Administrative costs associated with divestment may, however, be an important burden.

Two options exist for finding suitable buyers in divestment cases: a demerger whereby the company is split into two or more parts, or a management/leveraged buy-out. In the first case the original shareholders now own two sets of shares. Benefits may accrue both to the shareholders who are now able to alter their relative holdings in each part of the de-merged firm and to society from the resolution of an anti-trust problem. Further, it now provides the stock market with the ability to allocate capital between the parts individually rather than as constituents of a larger whole.

The management buy-out option is of particular interest, given recent developments in the capital market that have led to the financing of larger deals.[2] Management buy-outs demonstrate the feasibility of breaking off smaller parts of firms as viable entities, which by being independent avoid the anti-trust issues that might arise if they were sold to a new parent. The sale of Mecca Leisure by Grand Metropolitan in late

[1] For a review, J. Coyne and M. Wright, *Divestment and Strategic Change*, op. cit.
[2] J. Coyne and M. Wright, *Management Buy-outs in 1985*, op. cit.

1985 illustrates the potential of this route. If, for example, Mecca had been bought by the Rank Organisation, the deal might have been referred to the MMC. Sale to management avoided the delay and uncertainty of an MMC investigation. There may be good reasons why this option can be used as a tool of enforced divestment policy. Potential problems include the ability of management to run an independent entity; the role of financing institutions; the size of the leveraged package; the price that has to be paid; and developments following the buy-out. Where managerial skills are non-specific, replacing the weak elements in a team may be feasible. The narrow dispersion of shareholdings and the bonding commitment by management may help improve performance (though it is possible that performance may be constrained to meet short-run objectives and a desire by institutions to minimise downside risk). A highly geared package places a substantial burden on cash flow and may adversely affect investment activity, particularly if profit streams do not turn out to be as stable as forecast and unexpected investment opportunities present themselves.

The higher the price paid, the more of a burden will be the financing package. As noted earlier, the ability of corporate bidders to pay in paper may increase the price that management has to pay to acquire the company. Finally, at some time both management and financing institutions will seek to withdraw from the company. Where this involves a trade sale, the initial divestment problem may merely have been postponed.

Merger policy guidelines

UK merger policy is also criticised on the grounds that the criteria for reference are uncertain, and there have been calls for the introduction of guidelines such as those which form part of US policy.[1] The 1984 US Merger Guidelines use a series of price-based tests to determine the relevant market. These tests involve estimating what would happen if the firm imposed a small but significant and non-transitory increase in price (usually assumed to be an increase of 5 per cent sustained over one year) for each discrete product of the firm.

[1] For example, K. D. George, 'Monopoly and Merger Policy', *Fiscal Studies*, February 1985, pp. 35-47, and J. A. Fairburn, 'British Merger Policy', *Fiscal Studies*, February 1985, pp. 71-81. The US Guidelines are contained in publications by the US Department of Justice in 1968, 1982 and 1984.

Having defined a product market, the Justice Department identifies the firms that supply the relevant product and then uses measures of market concentration to reflect the likelihood that a merger will encourage collusion. The Guidelines also list a number of non-structural factors which are to be examined in considering a merger's likely competitive consequences. Such guidelines are not wholly satisfactory and they have always to take account of changing circumstances.[1] Nevertheless, the provision of some form of guideline appears preferable to the current British policy, and as Fairburn argues:

'. . . there would appear to be three main advantages to the adoption of merger guidelines. First, they would make explicit market share considerations which are now either implicit or vague. Second, they could introduce more rigour and predictability into analysis of market definitions, entry conditions and cost savings. Third, and perhaps most important, they would make the referral process systematic and thus ensure that any current anomalies in making references to the Commission would be ended'.[2]

The introduction of guidelines would significantly reduce the number of eligible mergers unless small increases in concentration, or market-share thresholds much below the current 25 per cent, were adopted. Such a step would also help to maintain competition in the market for corporate control. There is little evidence to suggest that removing many more mergers from the policy net would have any harmful effect on the public interest. Recent events, such as the Hanson Trust/United Biscuits/Imperial and Argyll/Guinness/Distillers bids, have emphasised the flexibility of current policy, and the willingness of the Office of Fair Trading to accept divestment of some parts of the company as sufficient to ensure that a reference will not be recommended. Such a move is a step in the right direction in that it recognises the fluidity in the corporate organisational structure and the scope for the sale of assets.

This informal procedure could benefit from being strengthened particularly to ensure adequate provisions if the divestments are not carried out. A suggestion here would be to extend

[1] For example, the discussion of the introduction of foreign competition into the 1984 Guidelines in A. F. Abbott, 'Foreign Competition and Relevant Market Definition Under the Department of Justice's Merger Guidelines', *Antitrust Bulletin*, Summer 1985.

[2] 'British Merger Policy', *op. cit.*, p. 80.

to mergers the 'Silent Revolution'[1] which has taken place in other aspects of competition policy. Mergers which meet certain criteria set out in any new guidelines, could be considered to be potentially an anti-competitive practice as applies to other activities of existing firms under the 1980 Competition Act. As such the Director General of Fair Trading would be required only to report on the competitive aspects of the merger. If there are no anti-competitive effects, a reference would not be recommended. At this stage, potential harmful effects on competition could be removed by agreed divestment which would have the backing of compulsion if not carried out within a suitable time-period following the completion of the merger. A finding of anti-competitive consequences would, on the other hand, lead to a recommendation to refer and to an analysis by the Monopolies Commission which would allow other considerations to be taken into account.[2] Such a change would preserve the basic elements of the case-by-case approach which is one of the strengths of British competition policy,[3] whilst clarifying the grounds on which reference is made. It would emphasise the role of competition in markets and make formal the current informal guidance which is given to companies by the Office of Fair Trading.

[1] D. P. O'Brien, 'Competition Policy in Britain: The Silent Revolution', *Antitrust Bulletin*, Spring 1982, pp. 217-40.

[2] In the view of the authors the Director General should be allowed to make direct references to the Commission on mergers without the necessary agreement of the Secretary of State, thus putting mergers on a consistent basis with dominant firms and anti-competitive practices in general.

[3] For arguments in favour of the case-by-case approach, M. S. Kumar, *Growth, Acquisition and Investment, op. cit.*, and Alan Hughes, Dennis C. Mueller and Ajit Singh, 'Competition Policy in the 1980s: The Implications of the International Merger Wave', *op. cit.*

TOPICS FOR DISCUSSION

1. How does the wave of merger activity in 1986 differ from those of earlier periods in the UK?

2. Why might a firm prefer to grow via merger, rather than by internal means? What problems need to be weighed in making this choice?

3. Who benefits from mergers?

4. Can insider trading be said to have any positive effects?

5. 'It is not so much *actual* mergers that are important for efficiency, but the *threat* that they may occur'. Explain.

6. Discuss the proposition that there is too much emphasis in financial markets on short-term performance at the expense of greater longer-term benefits.

7. There is currently a great deal of re-positioning by firms in the personal financial services sector. What might be learnt by firms in this sector from the experiences of mergers in industry generally?

8. 'This year's acquisition is next year's divestment'. Discuss.

9. Analyse the problems involved in introducing divestment deals with the OFT and enforced divestiture as part of merger policy.

10. Assess the case for mergers being required to show positive benefits to the public interest before being allowed to proceed.

FURTHER READING

GENERAL OVERVIEW OF MERGERS

Mueller, D. C. (ed.), *The Determinants and Effects of Mergers*, Oelschlager, Gunn and Hain, Cambridge, Mass., 1980.

Hannah, L., *The Rise of the Corporate Economy*, Methuen, London, 1983.

Cooke, T. E., *Mergers and Acquisitions*, Basil Blackwell, Oxford, 1986.

REVIEW OF THE EVIDENCE

Coffee, J., L. Lowenstein and S. Rose-Ackerman (eds.), *Takeovers and Contests for Corporate Control*, OUP, 1987.

Jensen, M. C., and R. S. Ruback, 'The Market for Corporate Control: The Evidence', *Journal of Financial Economics*, 1983.

Keown, A. J., and J. M. Pinkerton, 'Merger Announcements and Insider Trading Activity: An Empirical Investigation', *Journal of Finance*, September 1981, pp. 855-69.

Knoeber, C. R., 'Golden Parachutes, Shark Repellents and Hostile Tender Offers', *American Economic Review*, March 1986, pp. 155-67.

Cowling, K., *et al.*, *Mergers and Economic Performance*, CUP, Cambridge, 1980.

Competition and Merger Policy

George, K. D., 'Monopoly and Merger Policy', *Fiscal Studies*, February 1985, pp. 35-47.

Pickering, J. F., 'British Competition Policy on Mergers', *European Community Law Review*, 1980.

RECONFIGURATION OF ASSETS

Arrow, K., *The Limits to Organisation*, Norton, New York, 1974.

Wright, M., and J. Coyne, *Management Buy-outs*, Croom-Helm (Paperback Edition), London, 1986.

Coyne, J., and M. Wright (eds.), *Divestment and Strategic Change*, Philip Allan, Oxford, 1986.